# Ukrainian Knights

# Ukrainian Knights

*(An American Exodus)*

## Thomas Ed Posey

*AuthorHouse™*
*1663 Liberty Drive*
*Bloomington, IN 47403*
*www.authorhouse.com*
*Phone: 1-800-839-8640*

*Published by AuthorHouse    04/19/2012*

*ISBN: 978-1-4685-9534-5 (sc)*
*ISBN: 978-1-4685-9535-2 (e)*

# Contents

# *DEDICATION*

"To Erin and Matt, my favorite children"

# *Prologue*

---

*America's greatest living poet, Maya Angelou, once said,* **"Americans mistake making a living for making a life."** *Bravo, bravo, bravo, Maya! Her one simple declarative statement sums up so beautifully what will take me about two hundred and fifty pages to say. That's probably why she's Maya Angelou and I'm not. I consider myself to be in fast literary company just mentioning her name in my pathetic rag of a book. However, our messages are essentially the same. I realize of course that it is somewhat shameless to drop a great humanitarian and poet's name to somehow try and elevate my mindless drivel to her level of eloquence. But, you should also know that I have no intention of letting that shame stand in my way of writing this book. Whereas, her brevity of speech is succinct, and admirable and profound; my diatribes are pompous, plodding, arrogant, sometimes long winded, frustrating and occasionally maddening.*

*You should hear what my critics have to say about me.*

### Door number one or door number two

*You have two choices: you can either take this book in the spirit I intended, as a direct challenge to your American sensibilities, and resolve to change your attitude and, indeed, start making a life instead of just making a living . . .*

### Hey, America, your mama's so fat

*Or, you can take it as an insult and personal affront to your American sensibilities, labeling me as a fringe, radical, reactionary right wing nut-job and continue on with your pointless, meaningless, fruitless, silly, mundane little lives, until one day having arrived at your departure point from this life, you will have discovered you have never really accomplished anything, done anything or even particularly enjoyed the life you had.*

*The choice is yours.*

*I am an expatriate in training.*

*I spend part of my life in the Ukraine, part of my life in America.*

### The big dogs

*While I'm certainly no Fitzgerald or Hemingway, (fellow writers who lived in Paris but wrote about American themes back in their day), I'm not chopped liver either.*

*I don't pretend to lay claim to being a poor man's F. Scott Fitzgerald. Maybe I could be the anemic, drunken, totally withered shell of a writer, F. Scott Fitzgerald was in his last days. I think that sums me up quite nicely. Don't hate me for being an expatriate. I'm just on the voyage of self-discovery (I must admit I never knew what people were talking about when they said they needed to discover themselves, I thought it was just an excuse to twist off, or avoid a nagging wife) we all embark on in life.*

*Well, I do know.*

*And discovering oneself as I've subsequently learned, is the only reason, (other than raising children) you are here. Acceptance is the key. I know that it is a little bizarre to travel almost ten thousand miles to discover oneself.*

*I think my life compass has lost its polarity from time to time.*

*I figure its better that it happened somewhere in any time period, rather than the alternative, which is never. I am just fortunate that my journey has taken me to a few more interesting places than most people's journey has.*

*And you are fortunate enough that you get to vicariously experience what I did.*

### You like me; you really, really like me

*So, while I don't want you to hate me, you don't have to love me either. I am not proud of the fact that I spend so much of my time living in my adopted homeland, the Ukraine. But, I am not ashamed either.*

### My name is Bond, James Bond

*I'm certainly not over here hob-knobbing with ex-KGB agents, learning techniques (ala, Lee Harvey Oswald's assassin training; for you idiots out there, he lived in Russia, and then subsequently assassinated our president. Do I have to connect the dots?) and picking their brains on how I can (if I return to America) overthrow our government. I'm completely harmless. I know that sounds ridiculous to you, but some people in America have actually voiced the opinion to me that it would be impossible to completely trust a Russian/Ukrainian girl because you might never know for sure (well, maybe when she slips you the cyanide pill and life is oozing from your body, you would) she was a spy who was merely using you to gain entry into our country. The fact that any person living in America in 2012 (long after the Soviet Union even ceased to exist as a country) could still be so heavily influenced by propaganda and misinformation from such a long time ago is beyond astounding.*

### Please, God, not the KFC or Coke recipes

*What precise information would a spy steal from us that they wouldn't have access to in the first place? Good grief, (not that they need them) but they can get the plans on how to build an atomic bomb from the Internet. Or if they don't want to go to all that trouble, they can just ring up the Chinese or the North Koreans; they'll tell them what they need to know.*

*Spy on America? How Ridiculous!*

### I hope the spy stays out of Wal-Mart, lest she thinks all Americans are retarded

*How could any civilized country be that desperate?*

*Like most of you, the first forty years of my life were spent in strife and warfare; spiritual, domestic and personal, Some of this strife I surely brought on myself, but certainly not all of it. I want the next forty to be peaceful.*

*I'm not that much different from any other American. Those of us who have been around long enough to know that America is in a state of moral, economic and social decay (it ceased being a decline a long time ago), know the truth. You don't think so? Crap! Aren't reality television shows the most popular genre of shows on television right now? They're perverse and they're perversions, contrary to society's goals. Do you really want to keep sending the message to pre-pubescent and adolescent children that it's ok to eat a living thing or a pile of shit for money? Really? As long as what you are doing is for a great gob of money, nothing is taboo. Reality shows are popular because really beautiful people are being degraded and humiliated, and average looking people like that.*

### God, I miss Eddie Haskell

*Do any of you remember the fifties (before America got polluted and diluted with hedonism and greed, and became morally bankrupt)) and shows like "Leave It to Beaver" and "Ozzie and Harriet"? They were morally decent shows that had functional families and wholesome role models.*

*A recent study determined that only three out of twenty prime time television shows were suitable for "family" viewing. So, eighty five percent of the shows on television today are unsuitable for family viewing? Eighty five percent of the shows on television model either bad values or irresponsible behavior. Interesting.*

*There was a time in America when all of the shows on television had to be suitable for family viewing.*

*Isn't it strange how someone elected to call this specific genre of television, reality shows? Whose reality? Is that how you manage your day-to-day reality of living? The people on these shows have to engage in unbelievably underhanded and deceitful tactics to "win" the big bucks. By all means let us model this deceitful behavior for our children to view. Pay attention, kids, if you just learn how to gain the trust of other people and form alliances with them like the contestants do (and then break them at the appropriate time when it can do you the most good) you can be rich to.*

*These shows are catering to the lowest common denominator of humanity. Forty years ago, if you had aired a reality show like the ones on television today, they would have sent the producers of the show to prison for broadcasting indecent and obscene material. No, I'm not exaggerating in the least.*

### You talking to me? Are you talking to me?

*And the fact that you think I'm the one with the problem shows you just how bad things have gotten in this country, and just exactly what a curious point in history which we have arrived at.*

*I'm not certain about many things in life, but I'm fairly certain, I won't change any of your minds out there about how you live your lives or about convincing you just how pathetic our popular culture has grown in the eyes of the world.*

### Culture in decline? No shit!

*In the world community, America is like that sad/pathetic uncle every family has, (that's lost his way in life, been beaten down) the one they make fun of when he's not around. Let's be honest, most of you don't really care about the direction this country is heading or the legacy you are leaving your children, do you? As long as you have a case of a beer iced down each night and the remote control in hand, how could life be any better?*

*So, it's no secret then why children in this country behave like they do and why they seem fixated by nonsensical entertainment, phony celebrities and mind-numbing music.*

*Reality shows are only the tip of the iceberg.*

*Please understand that in order to make my point I have to engage in some broad-based generalizations. If you never allowed your child to watch anything but "Sesame Street" and The Muppets during his formative years, and you diligently read the classics to him while symphonic music filled the living room and if your child subsequently grew up to graduate magna-cum-laude from medical school, and he or she is now in sub-Saharan Africa fighting against all odds and time to save the natives from the ravages of Aids while alternating weekends being a nuclear (or as George Bush likes to say, nucular) physicist and a test pilot, I'm not talking to you!*

## *Decadence as a lifestyle decision*

*People, Americans are essentially good, God-fearing people. We are no different than any other affluent country in history that is in the last stages of civilization. Our culture has degenerated past the point of no return, past the point of salvation.*

*Of course, I'm not happy about it. Too much of anything is only a good thing for a while.*

*How did all of the great civilizations in the world fall? Almost indentically to America as a matter of fact: widespread civil unrest, apathy, branching out in cultural, social and economic imperialism (where they shouldn't, forcing one-time allies to take action against them) unchecked spending, complacency and misogynation.*

*Sound familiar?*

*The snake rots from the head down. There will be a catastrophic economic collapse in our near future. The one in 1929 was the baby, the precursor to the monster our generation will experience.*

*You think not?*

*How about the Soviet Union spending itself into economic oblivion? People, they aren't even a country anymore.*

*We have wasted a concomitant amount of money on the same type of military hardware. Of course as of press time we're still the United States of America, but even the North has been rethinking it's position of fighting to keep the Southern states in the Union the next time around.*

### We have met the enemy, and it is us

*Never, never, never forget who thine own true enemy is: yourself . . .*

*You will always be your own worst enemy. Accept the fact, embrace it, and now work hard to overcome it. Open your mind, and open your heart.*

*You can do it if you want to. If you decide to travel abroad, I can give you some things to think about.*

*I must point out a useful exercise to you. You must find out what your strengths and weaknesses are before you go abroad and attempt to interact with civilized peoples. I don't believe that most people (including women and girlfriends) consciously seek out your unprotected flanks, or your soft underbellies.*

*Your Achilles heel will rear its ugly head in its own time.*

*I know it isn't easy; I was no different than any of you are now. My sensibilities were strictly American, strictly provincial.*

### The truth! Novel idea, or antiquated principle of our forefathers?

*A man who constantly lies to his girlfriend for whatever reason, will eventually trip over his tongue. A man who is a philanderer, will eventually trip over his, well . . . you get the point.*

*In cultivating relationships, (especially with Ukrainian girls), lose the bullshit. Lose the swagger.*

*Out-smarting them or fooling them isn't going to be an option available to you.*

## Who were you expecting?

*The arrogant American.*
*The mistaken notion that we are smarter and better than everyone else in the world is preposterous.*
*People should strive to emulate us, right?*
*Ukrainian girls will see through your lies, like Kreskin reads minds, with ridiculous ease. And if you think you can fool these girls into believing something that is not true, you are either, (a) young and dumb or (b) old and dumb. The former is acceptable, the latter is not. I have many wonderful traits, I'm really a great guy, but I am prone to being emotional. You never have to wonder how I'm feeling; I wear my emotions like a cheap Halloween mask. (easy to see through). My enemies might say that I'm temperamental. My friends might say I'm just a little sensitive, a tortured artist. Well, that does have a much nicer ring to it. It does me no good to suppress my nature, or to try and pretend that I am not an emotional creature. I can't fool anyone; neither will you.*

## For thy lies are like a fire that consumes thy spirit

*Which isn't an actual verse from the Bible, but should be.*
*I know of half a dozen or so men who tried to tell some variance of a white lie to a Ukrainian girl; they all got caught.*

## Which is never a good thing

*The moral of the story is to know yourself and for the love of Krushchev, don't lie. I've had monkeys fly out of my ass more times than I've ever gotten by with a lie.*

## Which would be any video that featured a "noseless" Michael Jackson

*Modern society has environmentally programmed negative behavior into children patterns. Look closely at the stimuli they have in their environment: incredibly vulgar, visceral video and music imagery. If an impressionable child hears the lyrics of a song that tells him to go kill someone or commit suicide often enough it will eventually sound like a pretty good idea to some kids. Michael Jackson's life story is probably the single best commentary on American culture I have ever seen.* **Surely, only** *in America, could a poor ugly black boy grow up to be an average-looking rich white woman, and subsequently be a much adored pop icon based in part on his/her gender transformation. In Russia, (to deter others from doing the same thing)) they would drag someone like Michael Jackson into the street and beat him to death.*

*Pop culture is nothing but lies.*

*If you work hard like (fill in the blank here with the name of a pop star) you, to, can be famous. Really? Even if you are a hundred pounds overweight and buck-toothed? America is a country of almost three hundred million people with maybe a couple of thousand real celebrities. That sure doesn't sound like good odds to me.*

## Sieg heil

Our role model and expert on the subject of lying is Hitler, who said, "Repeat a lie enough times and it becomes truth." If you put enough crap into a developing child's brain, you are going to reap crap someday. Crap in, crap out! Surely nyet?

Surely duh!

## Sorry, Uncle Milty

Welcome to the television generation.

How do you like how things have gone so far? Kids flip though channels on their televisions (never in recorded history has an object been so adequately characterized as a boob tube or idiot box) like nervous addicts looking for the next hit of their favorite narcotic. I know television is an awesome baby-sitter. I understand that. But did you really think there would never be any consequences to the practice of children indiscriminately watching television? Really? Fascinating.

## The truth only hurts until it stops hurting

Look, you can pooh-pooh, or rationalize, or deny, or project your pissiness at me all you want. Facts are facts. They're certainly not my facts. Don't you know that the best medicine is always the most bitter? Kids are presented so much more audio and visual stimuli than their brains can process that their circuits can't help but get overloaded. Kids are desensitized to beauty, emotions, art *and anything that appeals to their affective predispositions. Some of the consequences are, but not limited to; anxiety, petulance, impatience, frustration, hostility, aggression and dissatisfaction with their own lot in life. How many times does a person have to see "Lifestyles of the Rich and Famous" to get the idea their life is basically dogcrap?*

## Ethel, why is our living room full of turds?

*America is a giant cesspool. You are living knee deep in shit but yet you still claim you can't smell anything. Really? How deep does it have to get before you think you will be able to smell it? I do love America. Although I'm sure you're having a hard time finding the love. Whether you believe that or not, I don't care. Just because a lot of things really piss me off about America doesn't mean I don't love this country. Are any of you out there married? I'm sure you all love your husband or wives, but I would bet my entire fortune against one dollar, that your spouses upset the snot out of you occasionally. I mean, I love fried chicken, too, but I hate greasy fingers. The good and the bad in life are supposed to balance out. I don't hate America; however, I do find our national attitude, tasteless comedy and overindulgence of children, quite despicable character traits.*

## Monkeys on your back, my ass, try elephants, America

*America is a great beast of burden that has been forced to endure carrying too heavy of a load, for too many years, until it finally collapses from overuse and excess weight.*

*The social ills (poverty, ignorance, illiteracy, alcoholism, promiscuousness, slothfulness and, racial strife) that beset this country are laughably obvious to all but the most ardent patriot and ostrich. The only difference between me and most of you, is that I'm not afraid to speak the truth.*

### Sadly, in America if you tell the truth, it will sound like Hell to a lot of people

*Harry Truman (who was noted as being one of our more cantankerous and acid-tongued presidents) was once asked by a reporter, "Why do you give so many people Hell"? His response was, "I don't give anybody Hell; I just tell the truth and they think it's Hell"!*

*Most of you (and maybe rightfully so) are afraid your neighbors might poison your dog if you say America is not the greatest country in the world. Please understand that I am drawing a clear distinction between a country's cultural standing in the world order and its position of power. America is unarguably and unquestionably the most powerful country in the world by virtue of the Soviet Union's implosion. The United States doesn't have a cultural standing at all. The historical record is also clear and unchallenged on America; from being the progenitors of the Industrial Revolution to the space race to the nuclear age. This record doesn't even take into account our engineering and technological innovations and marvels. America has dominated the world for over a hundred years.*

## *Or maybe no sense at all*

*Some things I will tell you may seem incongruous or immaterial. Trust me, it will eventually make perfect sense. And, perchance, if you don't get the message, don't feel bad. You are just at a different point in your voyage than I am. I just got there a little sooner than you. I realize not all of you will become true believers after reading my book. Fine, all of the turtles can't make it to the water.*

## *I'm a poor man's Jacques Cousteau of the literary world*

*I save what I can.*
*I'm like the starfish flinger.*
*A story; due to an unfavorable tide, thousands of starfish were stranded on a beach somewhere. A little boy was picking them up one by one and hurling them far into the water. An old man walked by and told the boy he was foolish.*

*There were thousands of starfish on the beach; he couldn't possibly make a difference. The boy, unperturbed, picked up another starfish, held it in front of the old man and politely responded. It makes a difference to this one, and flung it into the water.*

## *How do you really feel?*

*I understand completely that your natural response to what I am writing (having your foibles and societal and cultural inadequacies thrown into your face) will be venomous. They were my foibles to.*

*You probably consider what I am writing to be bosh mixed with hot air and sour grapes. Yum, sounds delicious. I won't hold your reactionary positions against you, because I know that I would have reacted in the same way if I, too, were the victim of information insufficient to formulate an educated opinion.*

### Trust me; ignorance "can" be total bliss

*I will probably tell you more about myself than you need to know. But I would rather err on the side of caution and give you more information than you need because I really, really, want you to understand why I did what I did. Some things I include for the fun of it. But there is a goal in there somewhere. There is a bigger picture to be seen. I hope my so-called writing style (sort of a flowery prose stream of consciousness) doesn't distract or confuse you. But, I f you are like most Americans (myself included,) the distractions are probably a good thing.*

# Chapter One

## Welcome to Western Siberia

*Even by the impossibly high standards of an unabashed beautiful dreamer, this romantic adventure, stood out. No small feat if you think about it. I had never been able to conjure up (on any subconscious or conscious level for that matter) even the tiniest of visions of what lay in store for me. Which is an incredible thing in itself because I'm known for conjuring up beautiful dreams. Maybe I never ever see any of them to fruition, but at least I'm an excellent conjurer.*

*For all intents and purposes, I was a modern day Rip Van Winkle. Asleep my entire life, casually floating along on the existentialist dream world we call life.*

*Long ago my senses had grown dull (which I obviously couldn't have known at the time) to the newness of a first kiss, I was immune to the splendor and grandeur of towering architectural structures, the ecstasy of sipping tea with a exquisitely beautiful woman at a sidewalk café and unimpressed by monumental monuments. I was equally oblivious to the rawness of Ukrainian sunlight at four in the morning, unaware of the luscious cottonwoods raining down their perfect snow-like blooms landing ever so gently on the Dnepr River. Unaware of the pure energy and vibrancy of the bustle of a busy people who sadly have no particular reason to be busy, but move about mindlessly anyway.*

### Indifference masked in apathy

I possessed a general malaise about the real wonders that passed under my feet, over my head and in and out of my life every second of every day.

As Einstein once said, "There are two kinds of people; those who think nothing is a miracle and those who think everything is a miracle."

Boy, when I put it that way, it sure seems like I missed out on a lot of the good stuff in life.

It really is a peculiar aspect of humanity that we could have somehow started out our existence on earth as such inquisitive creatures, thirsting for new adventures, hungry to conquer all frontiers compelled to rise up against any adversity that flew into our faces. Our curiosity for the last couple of hundred thousand years is responsible for all sorts of cool things ranging from fire to rocket ships.

But, somewhere in time, somehow our nature changed . . .

### My kingdom for a recliner, and a cold one

We became a complacent people, and in our collective complacency, (the path of least resistance, I suppose) over time we began to revel in it and actually like the feeling, (somewhat like a fat pig on a summer day reveling in the mud). Until one day we finally became this metamorphosized (I doubt that is an actual word) complacent people. We'll never know why or how the change took place. We can listen to the analysts and the experts, the sociological anthropologists, the naturalists, and the evolutionary Darwinist's, but it's a fool's errand as a fellow favorite expatriate and friend of mine, Lance Morton, was wont to say. Or even the great Apostle Paul who declared, "*Some questions are unanswerable and past finding out.*" *Hey, don't let common sense and the fact that billions of people over the last few hundred thousand years haven't managed to do it bother you. It is natural human vanity that forces us to try and solve the eternal mysteries. I'm sure you know that, but I also know that because of a certain notion of intellectual determination and perceived supremacy over the natural and unnatural world, you won't be deterred either. So good luck! I'm even going to take a stab at it and I know better.*

*It was just* **too** *gradual,* **too** *imperceptible of a change.*

### The Bastards

*For example, pretend that you walk into your house and someone has changed the angle ever so slightly of a piece of furniture or adjusted a chair. You won't notice the change (no one would) and there isn't even a good reason to notice. Until maybe one day your entire home has been rearranged and* **then** *you notice. But you couldn't possibly notice while the process was going on because it was too gradual.*

### Pay attention, you finally have to use your brains on this part

*Humans are loaded with so much pre-cognitive conditioning and such acute sensory deprivation of the brain that we never get to enjoy any of the real beauty that exists in the world. Our brains never stop filtering those things from the conscious world and subconscious thought that are illogical, irrational, or that don't fit our preconceived* notions. I can easily prove my supposition with a simple sentence: "I love Paris in the the spring" You didn't notice the second "the" in that sentence, did you? Of course you didn't. The subconscious part of your brain eliminated it from your conscious sight because it knew it was illogical. The sentence makes no sense with both of the, "the's." Then, it also follows that your subconscious brain filters things from the real world in the same way it does from written words. So your perception of things is never really perfect.

Our learned behavior and innate biological responses are self-limiting and create a finite world that we never really wanted to actually live in, (the world you wanted to live in, was the one we had as a baby (that you will never be able to retrieve) when we didn't know what was normal, or rational, or acceptable to the eye. It's just the world we are left with. Psychologists tell us that we create our own reality. That the life we lead is precisely the life we want. Why wouldn't it be? My God, we don't live in China or Chad or some other God-forsaken place where either human ideas ambition, or creativity are stifled, or the harsh poverty of the landscape holds us back. There are **no** excuses in America. No one could have stopped us from being whatever we wanted to be, if we really wanted to be this thing.

**Want happiness, true happiness? Listen to Don Henley every morning before you start your day. He's more spiritual, than any spiritual person you'll ever meet**

Don Henley, the smartest man that ever lived, or ever will live, said that we follow the wrong god's home. He's *right, you know. We've been following the wrong god's home for a long time in America. Stop doing that!!! Really! Stop!*

*It's silly and makes Americans look like bigger fools than we actually are.*


## We tried Slim Whitman tunes first

*I am not talking tongue-in-cheek about Don Henley. The rest of the world has already discovered what I'm trying to convince you is most certainly true. The first time I set foot in a foreign country (walking down a Vienna street), I noticed a street performer playing an acoustic version of "Hotel California."*

*In the next country I visited, the Ukraine, I was walking down a street in Dnepropetrovsk (on the second day I was there) and noticed another street performer playing "Hotel California" on a flute. The fact that street performers were playing "Hotel California" in different countries is not the main point. They do that merely for economic reasons. "Hotel California" is a recognizable song world-wide. Tourists are more likely to deposit some coins into the hat, if they hear a recognizable tune or maybe a song that evokes a certain homesick feeling inside of them.*

*If you look at the entire body of Don Henley's work, his songs touch on all subjects relevant to life in America. He sings songs which have a rare poignancy. He sings about the loss of loved ones, suicide, the joy of parenting, shifting cultural values in America, the inexorable passage of time, religion, and other intriguing subjects. Calling Don Henley a pop singer is like calling Jesus a carpenter.*

*Don Henley is the F. Scott Fitzgerald of music.*

*He knew things.*

*Each of his songs are miniature books which expound on a specific theme.*

*I'm not suggesting to you Don Henley is a God, even a little god, but Don Henley once said, "The biggest pile of crap ever perpetrated against humanity, was the notion that all men were created equal." God only created one Don Henley. No one else will ever be able to affect people and the world in general with their music the way he does.*

### *Faking it till they make it*

*I mean, for Pete's sake, I don't see other countries with false gurus like Koresh or Jones. I mean, sure they have Amin's and Khadaffi's and Ayatollah's and Hussein's and Bin Laden's, but they are hardly false prophets. With those guys, what you see may be crap, but what you see is what you get. What does that tell you? Without sounding like I'm beating a dead horse or even a slightly injured horse for that matter, there is no way to pinpoint in America when we decided that following the wrong gods home would be a nice change from what we had been doing. Although there have been evil acts (according to the Bible) recorded on earth since the beginning of human history, it wasn't that long ago, (my lifetime) your children would be safe if they stayed gone all day playing outside. Parents didn't worry and they had nothing to worry about. They knew their children would be back in time for dinner.*

### Carlsbad Caverns at night dark

*I don't know, people, but somewhere deep down where we all live, things got dark . . .*

*Real dark . . .*

*Maybe, just maybe, we are a restless people, the victim of our own wretched excess and luxurious life. We just don't know as a society (because we aren't technically a "society" like we once were) what we collectively want anymore. To me that's the rub of the thing. Not that life is so different than it used to be. Not that people are so different. Of course they are.*

*The rub is that I can't explain* **why***!!! Ugh!!! Things like that will disturb a genius like myself to no end. That we are willing to follow any god home that shows up on our doorstep that has a decent dental plan is infuriating, exasperating and wholly predictable.*

### Those of us who actually are messianic sure don't like those jerks who think they are

*From Jim Jones to David Koresh and all of the other demigods in between, we are mostly a* **lost** *people. Sorry, you don't have to agree with me; you have the option of being wrong if you so choose, but I guess you don't have to agree that the sun is a ball of fire in the sky either. And* **lost** *doesn't have anything to do with salvation, people. Lost is a condition that basically describes the current state of humanity. Our notions about eternity are somewhat amusing at best, downright goofy at worst. In one respect it is the greatest gamble ever conceived of by modern man. Behave myself and* **hope** *that I get an eternal reward. A* *definite possibility, albeit, maybe not a certainty; or stay in the flesh and hope I don't burn for eternity. The same possibility. Tough call, isn't it? Is it really?*

### Any of you ever go to Sunday School?

*The notion of right and wrong are absolutes, aren't they? I think hurting or killing people or stealing from them or not being willing to work or raise your kids in the way your human/animal instinct guides you, and to love the people who show you love in return are kind of universal themes. Secular themes possibly, although I'm no humanist . . .*

### Tough times don't last, but tough people do

*How was the last generation able to do so much with so little? How did they know exactly what they wanted out of life? They sure as hell didn't mind the sacrifices either. This country dominated the world because of them.*

### The sins of the baby boomers visited upon all humanity

*Unfortunately for humanity, the baby boomers allowed their drug-induced stupor, radical politics and undisciplined lifestyle to trickle down to their children.*

*So, the country isn't great because of anything that you or I have done.*

*I don't know the answers to all of the questions, just most of them. Anyway, my job is to ask the tough questions, not answer them. If I could do that, I'd have my own talk show instead of this book. There is a lot that can be said for careful introspection and looking backward (you certainly want to make new mistakes instead of the same old ones) so you can look ahead, and analyzing the totality of your life experiences. Then maybe you can get a decent bearing on which way to point your ship. But then on the other hand . . .*

*Colette said, "To understand life you must look backward, but to live life, you must look forward." Nice.*

*Of course, you can under-analyze things and never move out of your tracks . . .*

### Freud was gay and a pervert. Such venom!

*Some of you out there are probably saying all of this so-called analysis and psycho mumbo-jumbo is for the elite and privileged class, who have the time and inclination for such foolishness. Interesting. Although, in the interest of full disclosure Oscar Wilde did once say "the more you analyze people the more all reason for analysis disappears, and you are left with this dreadful thing called human nature." My god, I never noticed before, but doesn't "human nature" have sort of a nasty ring to it?*

### Captain, my Captain

*My favorite expatriate Lance likes to say, "I may go down, but I'm going to go down going forward." Without putting any words in his mouth, in my estimation, he is saying, "I'm not going out of this life with a quiet whimper.*

*I'm going to give it all I've got. I'm going to spend the life and energy force, that someone (God? Duh?) has invested in me, to do something."*

*America used to be a country of content souls. Do any of us seem content to you? I don't know any content people. Even our Pastor Jess, has ulcers and a nervous twitch Crap! You'd have a nervous twitch, too, if you had the same view he had from the pulpit every Sunday morning.*

### Are we there yet?

*So the journey begins.*

*It will be a journey through the heart of darkness and through a chasm of light. Like Martin Sheen going after Marlon Brando in "Apocalypse Now," there will be a lot of stops on the journey, some pleasant some not so pleasant.*

# Chapter Two

## The Awakening

*The anticipation was excruciating. It was almost cruel, almost brutal and almost sado-masochistic. I suffered through one entire year of waiting. I was waiting for the twelfth-hour reprieve from the governor to spare the executioner's blade. I certainly felt like a condemned man just waiting for someone to pull the switch on my last days in America. In some respects, life as an American makes me think of the supposition of doing things that we "can" do versus doing things that we "should" do.*

*If we, collectively as a society, can get everything we want and our heart's desire, should we? Hindsight, and a whole lot of living, has shown me, not necessarily. In America we all collect possessions for possessions sake.*

### Where's my slice of the American pie?

*The great lie in America is that more stuff will make you happier. Preposterous! In my life I've had no stuff, and I've had much stuff. Trust me, there is only momentary transient happiness to be found in stuff. I was happier, much happier, without the stuff.*

The second happiest day of my life, was buying my first new sports car. I imagine the happiest day of my life will be when I finally trade it in for a more sensible car.

There should be a sign that hangs in each of our border cities that reads, "Welcome to America, land of wretched excess, mindless activities, and disaffected children

Why are we like this? In Maslow's hierarchy of needs, even our poorest people have easily satisfied the home, food, safety, and warm place to crap, lower rungs.

So the simple to reason why we are like this, is because we can be.

### Make mine a red corvette

Most of us have skipped directly to the rungs where we have sports cars and spas. Once you get locked into this vicious cycle of acquisition of stuff, there is never a natural stopping point. You will be working for stuff and working to maintain your stuff your whole life. Your stuff owns you; you don't own it. In a country like the Ukraine, where almost no one has any stuff, they concentrate on the one commodity even a country in the direst of straits has, people.

In many European countries they have festivals (during the warm months) or some kind of celebration each week. They don't let the fact that they have nothing in particular to celebrate get in the way of a good festival. "Ok, what have we got this week, guys? Nothing! Crap, we've got to have something we can celebrate. Well . . . uh . . . how about, frogs? Excellent idea for a celebration; put it on the calendar!" Who among us doesn't want to celebrate the majesty, the wonder that is the amphibious frog?

*While it seems contradictory to say that in a country where the marriage rate is so low, and even in the healthiest of marriages, the guys keep something on the side, it is nonetheless true. They still focus on individual wants and needs and at least are willing to seek out meaningful relationships.*

*In America, if you are not a young man, and you are looking for a wife, you better have money. And vice-versa. It's just reality people. We are a materialistic, thing-oriented culture.*

## Show me the money

*There is a point that each person reaches in his life, when he is no longer willing to starve for love's sake. He wants to be fed and clothed well. And a sports car doesn't hurt either.*

*Wouldn't it be nice to just chuck all of this stuff that you won't be able to take with you to the afterlife and beyond anyway, and just live somewhere where nobody has stuff and you just learn a new way of living? Recapture the basic joy of being with your friends and walking in the park. In the warm months, Ukrainians go by the thousands into the parks every day to socialize and to experience the pure thrill of being outside in a pleasant environment. How often do Americans have three-hour dinners where they eat a little drink a little, and maybe dance a little?*

## Nice job, Sherlock, the last train just left the station

*Colette also said, "What a wonderful life I've had. I only wish I had realized it sooner." You will probably discover way too late in your life to do anything about it, that the best things in life really were free. Well, obviously not that last part; nice dinners aren't free. However, watching a burnt-orange sun slink below the horizon while holding your beloved's hand or watching your children play catch in the park or snuggling up on the sofa with your beloved, listening to some forties torch songs, are free. What are you doing with your lives, people? You grab something really disgusting to eat at a McDonald's on your way to a wrestling match a bass fishing tournament, a concert, a shopping mall, a sporting event, or some other mindless activity.*

*I almost fell over one day at my house. I turned on the television hoping to find an episode of "Masterpiece Theater", and much to my chagrin, I noticed that there was an interior shot of a coliseum somewhere. The people were going nuts, the spotlight was glaring and there were wide-eyed howling maniacs by the thousands. I was thinking to myself, what the Sam Hill have I been missing? This must be one big sporting event, as if I cared. The camera slowly panned down to some puny Asian guy standing on a stage with of all things, a fish in his hand.*

*Think about the imagery of it, people.*

*I once saw a puny Asian guy standing on a platform holding a fish in his hand while his worshipping minions howled their approval, as if he were a Roman gladiator who had just vanquished a ferocious competitor.*

*It was surreal. It was disturbing. It was tragically comical. It was very American*

*Now, I love to fish as much as the next guy, but I don't believe being able to put the right kind of bait on a hook to catch an animal as stupid as a fish qualifies me or anyone else for celebrity status. Fishing??? You cannot be serious.*

### Only dynamite would make it any easier

*They sit for hours on end on a padded chair drinking beer and casting out their lines. Besides what kind of idiot couldn't catch a fish with a twenty thousand dollar boat, five thousand dollars worth of electronic fish-finding apparatuses, (although not in competition) and hordouerves for bait?*

### Look, is it that hard to tell God from an impostor?

*Talk about following the wrong gods home. I have never been so ashamed to be an American in my life as I was at that moment. I have no words in my ample vocabulary to describe my disgust and humiliation at the realization that Americans celebrate fisherman as if they are real heroes. What next? Maybe we can go to events where people paint fences or wash our cars or cook hamburgers. My God, it's no wonder we are sometimes the laughing stock of the free world. I mean, do you see cultural centers like Prague, Paris, or Venice hosting bass fishing tournaments? For you rednecks out there, that was an example of a rhetorical question. Fishing tournaments on American television are just one more reason to live in Europe.*

### Keeping up with the Ivanov's

*If you can, just try and imagine a world where all that pressure to succeed and accumulate nicer stuff than your neighbors have would be gone.*

*So it was an interminable wait.*

*Like the first day of spring, which regardless of how close it seems, is always one more day away.*

### White Knight, Black Knight, your call

*If you were an almost middle-aged man about to embark on a mythical journey to a distant land, you'd be giddy, too. Like a knight somewhere out of time, seeking not so much to conquer a people, but to challenge the known world, (or at least, your known world) you would be excited, too. To finally see the world with fresh eyes, (not cloudy or half-closed) the way God surely intended you to see them with in the first place.*

### One pair of rose colored glasses please

*Maybe it's too simplistic an explanation or characterization of the trip. Maybe I have the narrow-minded view and the short-sighted approach of a man who is incapable of seeing things though unprejudiced or un-jaded eyes ever again. Maybe my thesis has merely stated the incredibly obvious and not the plain-vanilla obvious. Any number of you could surely put forth wise postulations to oppose my logic. We could get together and debate the topic and add our own spin to the subject ad-nauseum. You could* sing the praises of our free market economy and our vast wealth and incredible infrastructure. I would expound on the utter simplicity and beauty of living in a country where the pressure to be rich was gone, and the **people** are the economy of the nation.

## Actors say the darndest things

But in the immortal words of Gary Busey (just how many times has he fallen off his motorcycle onto his head anyway?), that intellectual giant and word-slayer, who was asked for a thought on Buddy Holly (the famous rock and roll singer who died tragically in a plane crash) said, "it just is."

What at first glance seems inconsequential and silly, in hindsight isn't so inconsequential and silly. If you somehow can do that, rationalize the intellectual part of your brain that knows certain things happen for no good reason with the emotional side of your brain that can be crippled by tragic and unpredictable events, (like Buddy Holly's death, or more precisely the death of loved ones) you can also conclude that some things "just are."

I suppose that in order to experience something beautiful or profound or emotionally pure you have to be in the right state of mind.

Trust me; you are not in the right state of mind now. I don't have to meet you to know that. Even if you meditated three times a day and went to confession four times a day, that wouldn't help you. You would still be an American with an American's perspective, pre-conceived thought patterns, and non-intellectual tendencies.

It's like trying to drive to a city you want to visit by avoiding certain towns that are directly in your path. You must pass through these towns to get where you want to be. There are no good short-cuts in life. There is mostly heartbreak to be found at the end of those roads filled with short-cuts. The obstacles in your way sometimes make your goals unachievable. Or sometimes, you must go through these obstacles to have a chance of getting to your destination. Having the singular American point of view is a mighty obstacle.

## To be or not to be

Your job will be to accept things that "just are," and it won't be easy. But, just because it isn't easy, won't make it any less worthwhile.

It's not easy to just cleanse your heart and your mind of the pain and the bad experiences in your past. They weren't put in their place overnight so they won't be easily dislodged.

## Did he have a way with words or what?

On one level, all you have is the past. As quickly as every moment of your life arrives, it recedes into the past. And to quote F. Scott Fitzgerald, "It eluded us then, but that's no matter. Tomorrow we will stretch out our arms farther, and one fine morning . . . so we beat on, boats against the current, born back ceaselessly into the past.

This line is arguably the single most powerful and poignant line in all of Western literature. It evokes such a feeling of longing, of wistfulness. It says so much about the human condition.

*We all romanticize the past to a certain degree. In our idle hours we replay the movie of our past in our minds. Over and over we replay the movie. Each time we get a little bit more clever, a little bit more athletic. The girls get a little prettier. Until one day the movie we play in our mind looks like either someone else's life or the Hollywood version.*

*Fitzgerald understood this.*

*What a waste.*

## Now it's up to me

*If he had lived twenty more years and not succumbed to a premature death of alcoholism, he would have changed the world, no doubt. Why? Because he wrote so eloquently and expounded so brilliantly on the human condition, that eventually even your run-of-the-mill idiots would have discovered that he "knew" things and he knew how to make you feel in ways no one before or since could ever make you feel. And that would have changed the way everyone approached living. Once "The Great Gatsby" achieved its number one status for Scribner's publishing house, it has remained there-unchallenged for over sixty years.*

*Fitzgerald new how to write about pain, he wrote that there was a special pain reserved only for those who are willing to love with all of their heart. Not only the part you are willing to share, but all of it. Which is all any of us are really willing to give-temporary conditional love.*

### Excuse me sir, would you kindly remove this knife from my back

*Oh, the pain of betrayal, of loss . . .*

I had nurtured my pain and cared for it like a miser polishing his gold coins. I wallowed in it and wrapped myself up more snuggly than a Sherpa with a single cotton sheet, camping without the benefit of a tent on the top of Mt. Everest.

### Mission impossible?

So the mission that I went on required that particular commitment. I summoned the guts to let it all go. So would you. Allow yourself to live again. The way God would have you live. Completely open to the notion of discovering the ever elusive concepts of love, beauty, and truth.

*The possibilities, oh, the possibilities . . .*

I hope I never run out of possibilities. Hope I never resign myself to a simpler fate. Hope that I never give up or give in some day; and that I make a conscious choice to live my life without the blinders. Try and take it all in, see what my life could be like, if I only had the courage.

### Clueless in America

Man, if you only knew what you were missing out on life, what wonderful experiences were waiting for you, you would probably put this book down and go book a flight. I wish I could somehow convey to you the reality of just how much bigger the world is than you ever thought it was. There is a stark beauty that exists in the world, a glorious undiscovered world full of wonder and awe. That is if you are up to the adventure. Sadly, for most of us, our precognitive thoughts, (the idea that we know everything we need to know, and there is nothing new to be learned) will limit the horizons that we are able to reach and completely and utterly define our boundaries. Like a beautiful fish swimming in a tank that never makes it to the ocean. It lives and dies in its miserable little tank and is fairly content about the whole deal.

### Pastor Tom Speaks

This next part is like a free sermon. It ties into my concept of what it important in life and how it relates to the decisions I make and how I feel about why we may have been put here.

### Just how many do-overs does God get?

My personal feeling is that God has a lot of other planets with a lot of other cool looking alien type life forms (of course to us they would be) in the universe who have not disappointed him as much as we have. Which serves as a possible explanation of why he has such a great fondness for them and His pronounced lack of attention to us? Look, for all we know he spends most of His time hob-knobbing on these other planets with aliens or monsters who actually know how to show some respect for the life He granted them. I'm not trying to be critical of God for his absenteeism; I'm putting the blame squarely on the shoulders of those who deserve the blame-humans, not God. But, it has been a few thousand years since God has made any special appearances or used His wrath or formidable powers of persuasion against us or for us in any comprehensible way. I'm certainly not blaming God for this prolonged lapse of time without any significant events like a good old-fashioned plague of locusts or a flood.

### Great, why can't I have a dream where I'm frolicking in whipped cream with Raquel Welch?

So, with this in mind, I fell fast asleep one night and in the middle of my peaceful slumber I had a dream. I was on the shore of a great river, I was just peering out over the water, and the sun was burning the expansive water to rippling silver waves. Marshmallowy clouds were over my head, like the ones I remember from my childhood when I use to lie on my back and try to imagine what beast or object they most resembled. I then saw a remarkable thing. A man was standing on the surface of the water. I thought that he must be standing in a boat, but he wasn't.

### Stop it already with the messiah complex

He started walking toward me. He seemed so happy. He was laughing and seemed to be thoroughly enjoying himself. He had somehow been able to conquer the metaphysical world, which no one else but Jesus and a few disciples had done up to that point, and he seemed quite pleased with himself. I was wondering how an ordinary man accomplished such a feat? The Bible says that anyone can, **if** they have the faith. That they could even tell a mountain to move, and it would, **if** they had enough faith.

So, if this strange man had conquered the metaphysical world, surely he had the "secret" to life. What if you are able to tackle a problem with the right set of eyes? Could you solve all of the mysteries of life yourself or walk on water? What if your happiness in life was only a matter of faith then? It is for the really special people, who have immersed themselves in the concept. I hate to break it to you, but the extent and condition of your faith is an unknown quantity, transient and elusive. Only when life and death scenarios enter your lives will you discover if you have any faith at all, only then.

### Tom's Sermon on the Mount

Aren't all the religious books that each faith holds sacred, man-made constructions? Divinely inspired? Maybe. I'm not saying they aren't. But actually written by God? I don't think so. Nobody (except for a few kooks here and there) thinks that. Think about it. All of our religious teachings expound on every topic and subject there is. For example, the Bible is an actual handbook on how to live. True enough. Not in any book, religious or otherwise, have we been told the actual meaning of life. Why? Man is in fact responsible for at least the production of all religious teachings. And MAN isn't God, so he doesn't know the answer. If you think you know the meaning of life, I guarantee you that you got the idea from a man-made source. That may be tough to swallow, but so was castor oil when you were a child, and look how good that was for you. Sorry. I wish it weren't true. But it is what it is. Physicists (I have a degree in Physics, too, so you'd better listen to me) know that in the absence of rational, logical, mathematical, (because the universe essentially, but not entirely abides by mathematical laws) explanations, the simplest explanation must be the correct one.

Which is not to say there aren't any definitive answers to the tough questions about life and the origin of man. We just need someone a lot smarter than any of us are, to answer them. If you are willing to admit only the facts into evidence, without editorial opinions you can come up with an answer, but is it the right answer? Maybe. I would argue that the greatest gift we have from God is (I am ambivalent [fence straddling?] about the trinity of God) is the gift of life. It is somewhat unreasonable in my estimation for the Father and Son to be one entity, believing in God should be enough. After all, God is Jesus if the trinity is accurate). I'm not pooh-poohing eternity, but in the Bible and every other religious doctrine we have, what is emphasized is what we do while we are here. You might argue against me that leading others to Christ or nirvana, being a martyr or simpatico with Mother Nature, or loving each other was the meaning of life.

Ok, maybe. It's not really my call to make. I leave the big stuff to the righteous people who are never wrong.

I have a hard enough time paying my cable bill on time without worrying about the really big stuff.


### God is infallible??? God meet Ross Perot!!!

God is too good to be unkind, too wise to make mistakes, and when I cannot trace His hand in my life I will search my heart to find His will. Spurgeon said that, not me. Hmm,

*Hitler wasn't a mistake? Interesting. How about Rush Limbaugh? No? Even more interesting.*

*I do know that a higher power had to put life (just think about a single DNA molecule, and how unbelievably complex, intricate and beautiful it is; DNA materializing from thin air would be like a Rush Limbaugh developing a personality while he slept) on earth because it is a factual* **impossibility** *that life could have somehow sprung from a soupy mix of gases and water and lightning. Doesn't that even sound ridiculous? Of course it's not true. I would more readily believe in ghosts and Rush Limbaugh finally giving up powdered donuts than that postulation. If spontaneous generation had any factual basis, it would be repeatable. Real scientists know this, but, due to their professional complicity and duplicity, they never bring it up.*

*Why??? It's the only lame explanation they have.*

*In my life experience, it's the only incidence I know of where I can incontrovertibly say that scientists intentionally dishonored the "simplest explanation postulate" when presented with conflicting or irrational information.*

*You cannot combine heat (the sun or lightning) and water and any type of gas (erupting volcanoes give off methane, which has carbon in it and life is based on the element carbon) in any combination and produce life.*

*The few scientists who have attempted such experiments produced only a couple of amino acids and tar, (a goolike inanimate substance), certainly nothing even close to the production of a living organism. Two amino acids is about forty short of a miracle. And these experiments were carried out under ideal atmospheric conditions (lots of methane), which have never been proved to have existed on earth, in the first place.*

*It's stupid goofy.*

*I weep for their ignorance, masked so brilliantly in arrogance and intellectualism.*

*"To believe that physical and chemical forces could by themselves bring about an organism is not only mistaken, but stupid." Shopenhauer, "In Parerga and Paralipomena."*

*"Science! Why preyest thou thus upon the poet's heart? Vulture, whose dull wings are reality.*

*Edgar Allen Poe.*

*Why do scientists make so much hay at the alchemists expense for trying to convert basic metals into gold (transmogrification), but embrace the foolish notion of the spontaneous generation of life from inert substances? Stupid goofy I tell you.*

### Daddy, was my Great, Great Grandfather really an amoeba?

*Not only shameful, but incredibly embarrassing!*

*But for you eggheads out there, modern humans have only been here a hundred thousand years or so (the fossil record irrefutably proves that) and the Earth is at least five billion years old, so something has been going on down here.*

*Well . . . What do you think was going on here for almost five billion years? Earth is after all a dynamic planet, unlike the other planets in our solar system which have long since been dormant. The other planets are essentially nothing more than either giant rocks or balls of gasses orbiting the sun.*

### *Hey, if a caterpillar can turn into a butterfly, I believe Rush Limbaugh has the capacity to turn into a human*

*The really funny thing is, I* **like** *Rush Limbaugh (he's right a lot more than he's wrong) he's just an easy target because he's so pompous and fat. He's the hobbled gazelle of political circles.*

*A lot of change, that's what was going on here. As much as I know that there is a higher being in control of things I also know that organisms and the earth have changed over the vastness of time. Just get over it. But these are only a few of the facts I know. A more definitive answer is out there people.*

*Maybe, there is a child somewhere in the world this very minute who will someday grow up to be that person, the one that puts it all together. The one who discovers some bit of archeological evidence or ancient religious scroll (manmade evidence?) that conclusively proves what the origin of man is, and who put us here and why. Will that not be a sad day? Life will no longer be a mysterious proposition. Life will be reduced to nothing more than one indisputable mathematical proof. Obviously, once the wheels of the universe were set into motion, natural laws have taken over. Or, as the great scientist Brian Silver once said (tongue in cheek I hope), "If God actually did exist, I like to believe she died giving birth to the universe." Well, however farfetched and ridiculous that sounds, it sure would explain a lot about what's been going on in the universe since that point in time.*

### You know it's pretty bad when a person can even distract himself

*We will lament that day; bitterly we will lament it.*

*But my main point (and that was a mighty long bird walk we took) is that your mind has to remain open to all of the possibilities. You have to stop walking around in your own little ecosystem, swimming in your private cesspool, wrapped up in a cocoon, virtually a self-imposed bubble. It's not entirely your fault, of course. I mean, you are what you are and believe what you believe because of who your parents are and where you were born in the world. Those are strong genetic and environmental prederelictions to have to overcome, and that's if you want to overcome them. Think about it (this is an observation, not a criticism for you fanatics out there), if you are a Baptist I can almost assure you your parents were Baptists. So, whatever Baptists believe, you are going to believe. Which has nothing to do with what is actually true or not true.*

### Nice try, Hoss, but no cigar

*Organized religions (all of them) are attempts at bringing order to the unorderable world, meaning to that which is unknown, and structure to a sometimes chaotic universe. Dinosaurs were after all wiped out by a meteorite collision with earth, which certainly qualifies as a random act of celestial violence perpetrated against the earth.*

*So, the notion that any given religion anywhere in the world has the answers to the meaning of life is childish and self-serving. Not yet. Of course they don't. You may believe in a lot of things, but you actually know almost nothing. Theories can only be disproven, never proven. The beginning of all wisdom is realizing you don't actually have any wisdom at all.*

*You have to be your own scientist. I've taken an unbelievable amount of verbiage to say this one thing that the finite is a bad world to live in. Don't do it. The world is waiting on you.*

# Chapter Three

## Once upon a time in the Ukraine

*The beginning of the rest of my life took place on a Sunday. On a Sunday unlike any other before or since this one.*

*My life was irrevocably changed.*

*For the better or the worse, is a question that can only be answered over time. God and time eventually reveal all truths.*

*Someone once said, "You will always remember where you were when you decided what you want to do with the rest of your life."*

*The plane dropped ever so slowly through the snow white clouds and steeply banked over the dark rich farm land far below me. I suddenly got a knot in the pit of my stomach. I finally, got my first real glimpse of what the Ukraine was going to be like.*

*My future homeland.*

### I guess a welcoming aloha dance and a lei, is completely out of the question

*The Dnepropetrovsk Airport was almost directly under me now. It was, well . . . how do I say this? Stark, bleak, ramshackle and bare-boned would be just too damn flowery of a description. I was getting tense faster than a Ukrainian cab backing down a four-lane highway. Yes, they do that, no shit! Hey! I've been known to drive my sports car fifty miles per hour through an automatic car wash and under speeding eighteen-wheelers, and that even scared the dog stuff out of me. Oh, yeah. It got worse. Once inside the bleak bungalow of an airport where I fully expected to see a sign saying "Welcome to Westen Siberia, (ok, maybe too much hyperbole) but believe me it was more destitute looking than a Ukrainian panhandler. Ok, I guess in order to get that analogy you would have to know that all Ukrainians are poor, so that a Ukrainian panhandler would necessarily be really poor. Oh, never mind. And, of course, the stereotypical story everyone knows about is that there is no toilet paper in Russia. Which, I subsequently found to not be true. But as fate would have it, and it always seems to have its way, the airport bathroom on this day had no toilet paper. And, believe me, I had already had the crap scared out of me and into my pants, so this was a little unfortunate. But I digress. I had already caught a glimpse of what the "customs" agents looked like. Think about every bad James Bond movie you've seen where the Russians are decked out in drab, shopworn, green uniforms and look completely humorless, cold, and cruel. Well, they weren't that pleasant looking. Scary, scary, scary people. I swear it's true.*

### Capone was right, you get so much more cooperation with a kind word and a Kalashnikov than just a kind word

*I honestly believed that at any moment one of them was going to shout instructions or orders at me in Russian, orders that I obviously was not going to be able to comply with (being a non-Russian speaker) and that a Kalashnikov was going to be whipped out and I was going to be dead. I didn't consider it to be a remote possibility at all. Oh, the horror of it all. What a cruel twist of fate to suffer, to travel all this way and then have such an untimely demise at the gates of paradise without setting so much as a toe in the promise land.*

*Their weary, haggard countenances honestly produced a real feeling of dread in your mind. Ok, I have a fairly active imagination, and the image of the stereotypical Russian that had been lodged in my mind since birth was possibly a superficial image I couldn't shake. However, real or imagined, I'm pretty sure they would have scared the poo out of most people.*

*While I'm on the subject of Russians, how about an observation? Well, actually a lot more than that.*

### America, love it or leave it

*It has to do with nationalism. I actually started out my college career as a Political Science major before switching to Physics, so I'm acutely aware of the root cause, the mechanisms, and the processes involved in the rise of nationalism in the twentieth century. It's a touch more complicated than this, but basically protectionist trade practices (Vern, them damn rice-eaters are gonna' send us to the stinkin' poor house if we don't stop buying them damn puddle-jumpers, and they don't start buying some damn Chevy's from us) and the fear of communism produced the rise of nationalism in this country. Other countries in the world have their particular reasons for the rise of nationalism (sometimes border squabbles or religion), but for us, that about covers it. Our last border squabble, was with Mexico about a hundred and fifty years ago, and I assure you that my friends and I have done our part to smooth over any lingering hurt feelings by furthering international relations and the cultural exchange between the two countries by visiting frequently. Mexico has really "nice" social clubs.*

## Canada, France of the New World

*Our border with Canada is the longest uncontested border in the history of the world, mostly because Canada is made up of a bunch of Frenchman, and France would roll over and play dead if Ethiopia invaded them.*

*So, you're going to have to do something really horrible to get Canada to fight with you.*

*From the time we were babies in America we had been taught that the Russians were a godless, cruel, unforgiving, humorless people. Some of them of course are, most aren't any more godless than Americans are. It wasn't accidental propaganda. It was an extension of the domino principle. My God, if the Communists take over South Vietnam what's next, Puerto Rico? Alaska? Hawaii? I mean, weren't they basically on our doorsteps like the school bully just waiting for us to step outside to give us an ass-whupping? Or maybe even come into our houses and give us an ass-whupping? Right.*

### They certainly didn't look any tougher than Grenada on paper

*Keep in mind; they did invade Afghanistan in the 1980's. So, the Soviet Union still had some fight left. Once again (like Vietnam), we fought a defacto war against the Soviet Union by lending military support to the Muhajadin, which enabled them to defeat the second greatest army in the world, the Soviet Army. Imagine it, bedraggled and disheveled camel-riding (huh)Afghan rebels overcoming the might of the Soviet military? It's almost inconceivable. Well, it's not as inconceivable as you might think considering we gave them hand-held missile launchers, (stingers) that enabled the Afghans to shoot down one piece of Soviet Aircraft a day, for over two months.*

*Don't' get me wrong, I am not one of the avowed dove people.*

### Steers and queers, which one are you, boy?

*Do not misunderstand me. I love a good scrape. Just like the old cowboy story of the big bull that always pawed the ground around the little bulls just to remind the other bulls who the biggest bull was. Sometimes a country like America has to remind the other countries that we're still a pretty big mamma-jamma bull when we want to be. All the little bulls better keep their asses off our porch. And if that means beating the Hell out of Grenada or Iraq, or some other third-world country that still has sheep and cows grazing in their biggest cities, then so be it.*

*Let me be the first person to say that Hussein got what he deserved, and Noriega and the Bosnian guy, too.*

*Truthfully, all of this American propaganda wasn't without **some** merit. After all, there "was" a time (the fifties) when the Soviet Union and its leader (Khrushchev) claimed they would bury us. Information gathered about Krushchev from the post Cold War era, has since proven this theory to be erroneous. He was all bluster and bluff. Having said this, I still don't think we were exactly being alarmists to stir up some nationalism and paint the bad guys as the bad guys.*

*They were bad.*

### Very nasty man

*Stalin (the leader before Krushchev of course) purged thirty or million of his law-abiding citizens in his reign of terror. Hitler could only dream of such carnage. How bad of a person was Stalin? A Russian professor told me that at the beginning of World War Two when his son (A second Lieutenant) was captured, the Germans sent a cable to Moscow indicating to Stalin that they were prepared to exchange him, for a captured German Field Marshall. Stalin's reply, I don't trade Lieutenants for Field Marshalls. And you thought you had a heartless dad. Stalin's "enemies of the state" were sent to gulags. Which were nothing more than glorified forced labor camps, for the express purpose of bringing the Soviet Union into the modern era. They were located mostly in Siberia. Escape meant certain death. The gulag era produced two irrevocable psychological schisms on the Russian mind. Firstly, a total and complete distrust of authority figures. In some of the flats I've lived in the Ukraine, there are three solid wooden doors you must breech to gain entry. Affording you plenty of time to climb out of a window, if the government comes a knocking in the middle of the night. Secondly, a belief that government must suppress individual freedoms, in order to survive.*

## I guess he didn't feel like being the Great Communicator on that day

*Yes, our government, i.e., Ronald Reagan, once called the Soviet Union the "Evil Empire", but hey, there is no Soviet Union anymore. And the new Russia isn't much more dangerous than a retired toothless, circus tiger. Hell, they can't even make the Chechnyans behave. I guarantee you the old Soviet Union would have gone into Chechnya with a tank division and a hundred thousand troops and Chechnya would have gotten their asses out of the terrorism business (blowing up planes, taking over movie houses, and murdering school children), and back in Sunday School. And they would have been happy about it.*

## Ooh, they kind of nailed us on that one

*Conversely, the Russians did the same thing to us. They used a cartoon character aptly named the "capitaleest" in the school primers. He was a fat, lazy, bald person. And the Russians made a lot of hay at the "captialeest" and America's expense. Their propaganda served the same function ours did: To coalesce the country into one view. One pristinely clear false image of the other guy. Except for obvious cultural differences, people are essentially the same everywhere. I said* **essentially**, *not exactly. For example, if you tell an Asian person he's no smarter than an American, he's going* *to beat the crap out of you. Well, that is, if he weren't so tiny, he would.*

### I'll show you my tactical nuclear weapon, if you show me yours

*Curiously enough, if not for the effects of Communism and Socialism, (and since we had the only intact economy after World War Two) they surely would have buried us a long time ago. Except we did have a three-pronged nuclear attack (land, air, sea) deterrence with the promise of mutual annihilation that effectively kept them at bay, and stewing in their own juices. Trust me, people, Russians are resourceful, highly intelligent, and will out-work even the most diligent American.*

*Do you have even the foggiest notion of how many trillions of dollars were wasted on the nuclear arms buildup and subsequent Cold War between America and the Soviet Union? I didn't think so.*

*It's ghastly.*

### Well, besides bailing Chrysler out it is

*It may be (I said may be) the greatest singular con job and crime by a government ever perpetrated against its people.*

*For what result?*

*Nothing!!!*

*To make matters even worse (and rub a big ole piece of salt into the wound), not only did we spend the trillions of dollars, we never got the thrills of an actual war?*

### Hey, fella, can you spare a few trillion dollars for a few tactical nuclear weapons?

*In the case of the Cold War, the Soviet Union (as I've already mentioned) spent itself into oblivion. What you don't know or realize yet, is so did America. We were at a different economic starting point than the Soviets (the war in Afghanistan did most of the damage), so it's going to take a little bit longer for the economic catastrophe to catch up to us. Don't worry, it will; it's only a matter of when, not if. Lest you don't believe me, pick up the latest economic diatribe du jour from your local bookstore, for confirmation of this belief.*

*Imagine if you charged several million dollars worth of clothes and jewelry and goodies for your home and kids on your visa card. You have about as much chance of paying off your imaginary debt, as our government has of paying off its real multi-trillion dollar debt. China could bankrupt us in one day by demanding payment of their treasury notes. Believe it!!*

*Except for a tiny point in history, the Cuban Missile Crisis (I even know a man who actually boarded a Russian ship to inspect it for nuclear weapons during the naval blockade of Cuba) there was never any real threat of nuclear war. I told you, it was an unwinnable war and both sides knew it. The Cuban Missile Crisis was yet another instance where America believed it could do as it pleased, and the world community (specifically the Soviet Union) would just have to take it. America objected rather vehemently to the Soviet Union having a few hundred nuclear weapons positioned in silos less than a hundred miles from its shore. While at the same time having even more nuclear weapons positioned in Turkey within the same striking distance of the Soviet Union, was just fine to us.*

*My friend told me what I already knew: it was propaganda that kept the Cold War alive after 1962.*

*I've participated in the mock scenarios of war games between us, and various superpowers dozens of times. The result is always the same. When reason fails and superpowers come to blows, there is never a winner. Mutual annihilation is always the end result. Limited mutal annihilation is a non-sequitor. Don't you think each respective government has played out the same scenarios in their war rooms thousands of times?*

### You know how much Generals love to play with miniature toy tanks

*Of course they have. The nuclear arms buildup had nothing to do with a real threat of nuclear war.*

*Politics and money friend.*

*Lots of it.*

*Trillions upon trillions.*

### And they will be headed for a disposal site near you

*We've dismantled most of those weapons we stockpiled, and the Soviet Union faded off into the history books. They went the way of the dodo bird. Do you realize what that money could have done to rebuild this nation's inner cities, fund public education, and maintain Social Security? Millions of senior citizens in this country are forced to live on a few hundred dollars a month in abject squalor because of the gross mismanagement of our country's financial resources by every administration since World War II. Whether they were Republican or Democrat is a moot point.*

*They were all insane.*

*How do you feel about America now? The very people who built this country into the massive economic superpower that it surely is are forced to live in poverty.*

*It's repugnant to me how generations of elected officials have been able to sell us down the road to financial ruin. Hey, don't blame them.*

### How did he know so much?

*President Garfield said, "Free market societies are ruled by the collective wisdom and folly of the people." Well, the folly of the American people is self-evident, but wisdom? When? Where? Even Walter Cronkite, once the most respected man in America, went on the record just recently and made the statement "That Americans are too ignorant to elect qualified leaders."*

### If you look up the definition of ironic in the dictionary this is the definition they give

*At the end of World War II, after the Soviet Union had lost twenty million of its citizens (12% of the total population) and 95% of its food production capacity was destroyed, and most of their cities lay in ruins due to the onslaught of the German army (which eventually was repelled by the Red Army's tenacity and the brutal Russian winter) General Patton suggested to Truman that we take out the Soviet*

*Union. His rationale, was either fight them now when they have basically lost the ability to defend themselves or fight them later after they have rebuilt their country and are once again a formidable, if not invincible foe.*

*However, at the end of the war there was widespread sympathy for the Soviet Union; they lay in ruins with twenty million fallen comrades, and they were, after all, our reluctant allies.*

*If they had not occupied so much of Hitler's resources, he surely would have come very close to conquering the world before we had the capacity to nuke Japan. We opted to help them rebuild their infrastructure and feed their starving citizens.*

*Now for the ironic part.*

*Once the United States helped restore the Soviet Union to its former position of economic and political preeminence, Krushchev (who succeeded Stalin) made a pronouncement that they were going to bury us! Which as it turned out, was just bluster. I don't know, it may just be me, but that seems a* **touch** *ungrateful. Not just biting the hand that feeds you, but actually tearing the hand off your master's arm and then making a snack out of it.*

*But enough rambling. I'm even making myself sleepy. I have given you a splendid history lesson and psychological analysis of the Russian people and the reasons for nationalism. The tale must begin sometime . . .*

# Chapter Four

# The Lost American

*The Ukraine.*
*Land of contrasts.*
*Land of mystery.*
*Land of danger.*
*Land of paradoxes.*
*Land of beauty, for sure . . .*

*Sounds like the opening of a National Geographic Special.*
*In the next couple of chapters I will more or less address these particular attributes of the Ukraine as they occurred to me.*

### Without the poodle skirts

*Going to the Ukraine is like going back to America with a time machine circa 1955. Now there's a happy thought for you. And I know what all of the femmi-nazi's out there are saying in unison. Right! Back to a time, when women were sex slaves and couldn't leave the house. And your point is? Just kidding.*

### Eminem isn't fit to lick Sinatra's shoes, even if Sinatra is dead

*A time when old world values were still in place. Before Kennedy got assassinated, illegal drugs took hold of our youth, and rap stars (white and black) who have no apparent musical skills whatsoever, became billionaires. I'm prejudiced, alright. I really don't like it when idiots or people with no discernible talent, get rich, do you?*

*It violates our pre-cognitive notion of fair play, and the prototypical American concepts of how a person should get to be successful.*

*So we have an understanding.*

*Modern day Ukraine is like America was. No morality judgment necessary.*

*It just is.*

*I need to give you my second impression of the Ukraine because I fear that my first impression of the airport personnel was slightly misleading. I truly believe the Ukrainians do that on purpose. Sort of like your high school teacher who gave you the blood and guts story at the beginning of the year of the child who messed with him or her, and they never found his body. They come with their "A" game to get their bluff in on you. So does the Ukraine. You think we're hard-asses at the airport, stupid American? We're the cream puffs, we're the ones with sugar in our britches, and we're the gay boys. Just wait till you see the real bad guys! So watch yourself, stupid American!*

### If the shoe fits

Get used to the stupid American moniker. Unfortunately, there is some justification for this vitriol. Generally speaking, Americans don't travel abroad inconspicuously.

### What's the matter for you, eh?

Other than Italians, who are just raving lunatics, Americans are the complainingest, rudest, most irritating travelers there are.

### Is there ever a good time to wear knee high black socks, with plaid Bermuda shorts?

I was visiting with an American airline pilot in the Vienna airport, and he said that he had traveled so much (like three hundred trips across the pond) that he could spot an American tourist from one-hundred yards away. Not good, people. That's just too conspicuous. People, you will never have things as well as you do (at least from the luxuries standpoint) in America, so you must factor that in before you travel overseas. You have to psyche yourself out before you ever board the plane. Lower your expectations and then stick to them.

I received my second impression of the Ukraine while riding in a mini bus through the streets of Dnepropetrovsk on our way to the hotel in the town square. The Hotel Central, of course. It was an assault on the senses. Obviously, being an almost third world economy with all that entailed, intermingled with ancient architectural buildings in an urban/rural setting (there were small vegetable gardens spread out in a city of two million people and farm animals grazing on the side streets) and then seeing modern dress styles was, well . . . a peculiar thing to see. But, maybe peculiar only because I had never seen it before.

I'm certain it's no more peculiar to me, than it would be to a Ukrainian who visits America and sees something close to the opposite.

## Twas the night before Christmas

All of the anxiety I had experienced at the airport was now replaced with a kind of nervous excitement. I was excited at the prospect of seeing things that I couldn't even have imagined (because in my mind I carried around too much bad imagery), but slightly nervous because I was a stranger in a strange land.

Unbelievably, except for a few notable exceptions such as architectural style and an ancient mass-transit bus system, you would be hard-pressed to illuminate the differences between downtown Dnepropetrovsk, and downtown Cleveland. The names of the shops that appear on the veneers are in English. Go figure. And Ukrainians certainly look like Americans in basic form and structure. We will discuss the differences in personalities soon. Be patient.

## Tom falls hard, real hard

When was the exact moment in my trip that I first realized that Dnepropetrovsk was the place I wanted to spend the rest of my life? Easy, comrades, in time. Lance *and I, along some other Americans were invited to a social (dance) on the Dnepr River.*

*The social was held in a large two story (first floor dining, second floor dancing) octagonal shaped Restaurant on a small peninsula that jutted out into the Dnepr River.*

*There were approximately twenty American guys entertained by over two hundred Ukrainian girls on this night.*

*With these odds, even I am likely to find someone to dance with.*

*It was early in the evening when we got there.*

*The restaurant was beautiful. I found most of the restaurants that I dined at in Dnepropetrovsk to be on the elegant side. They did not fit the stereotypical, bare bones, ramshackle image I had in mind. They were closer to Tavern on the Green, than the Sizzler. I walked up the stairs and looked out at the Dnepr River. I was awestruck. Imagine what the Mississippi River would look like if it were blue instead of brown and a whole lot wider.*

*The blooms were falling from the cottonwoods that lined the bank of the river. I could see from the veranda hundreds of people walking up and down the river bank going about the business of living.*

*Even if you subtracted the girls from the equation, I would have still had the same experience. It was a perfect moment in time. It was a confluence of many feelings and emotions, of hope and desire, of longing.*

*Finally, it was to be a shot at redemption for a mostly wasted life.*

*I had an overpowering sensation inside my head and heart. A feeling I had never had before.*

*I felt total peace.*

*Total bliss.*

*Total contentment.*

*I felt like I was home.*

*The thought struck me like a cannon ball in the groin, that I had wasted most of my life by not really doing what I wanted to do or living where I wanted to live. Yes, on some level the sacrifice I made was noble. I told myself that it was for my children, whom I dearly love. I can't count any days I spent with my children in America as wasted time and I never will. Although, I claim no right to martyrdom. Millions of people all over the world are perfectly willing to make the same sacrifice I made.*

*But, what is my excuse* **now** *for living my meaningless, joyless existence? Who do I get to blame now besides myself?*

*Sure, I was indeed overwhelmed by the moment and by my visceral surroundings, I understand that, but for me it was more profound than just the beauty of the moment. It went deeper than that.*

*Eventually, a day like the one I had, will eventually arrive in every person's life.*

*The day you stop lying to yourself and you start living your life the way you want to live it.*

*With no apologies or excuses to anybody!*

*Which doesn't mean you have to forsake anyone or leave anyone high and dry; you just have to be honest with your loved ones about what you want to do with the rest of your life.*

### Can a diet book be far behind?

*When I said that Americans and Ukrainians have the same basic form and structure, that was a little bit of an overstatement. Ukrainians are built like wild animals. They typically prefer low-fat food, and their food supply is not as contaminated as ours. They walk for miles and miles and miles. And the girls do it in heels. They are lean, muscular, physical specimens. Their American counterparts, while still technically in the same species, are . . . well . . . how about I just say, well-fed?*

### Alligator wrestling, anyone?

*This next bit of information, I give you solely and purely in the name of science. I am after all a scientist by nature and to not report this information would seriously affect my credibility as a man of science. Consider this to be the personal scientific/observer portion of my experiences. It involves the "romantic" aspect of dating Ukrainian girls. I should warn you, you've never experienced in America with "any" girl what you would experience in the Ukraine with a Ukrainian girl. Unfortunately, there is a constant danger of breaking a bone, tearing a muscle or dying, (in no particular order) while involved in shall we say, "romantic interludes" with Ukrainian girls. And from the information I've gathered (strictly for scientific purposes, I assure you) from different sources (because I was concerned my personal experiences were anecdotal and not empirical) was that it was fairly typical mating behavior. Yes, they are the second most passionate girls in the world, obviously behind latina women, but then again, all women are a distant second place to latina women.*

### *Hugh Hefner complex*

*Hugh Hefner may be able to service seven twenty-year-old American girlfriends and be no worse for the wear. But I assure you, he couldn't survive seven twenty-year-old Russian girls.*

### *Will the last single American man leaving America, please turn the lights off?*

*I can only hope that my next statement doesn't cause the airspace over the Ukraine to be clogged with lovesick Americans. I can just see dozens of airplanes crashing into each other because of the haste of the Americans to get there. The Ukrainian air traffic controllers still use binoculars and a board with miniature wooden airplanes to monitor air travel, so they can't exactly juggle a lot of planes at once.*

*Ok, I was joking.*

### *Andy Warhol was a prophet*

*My only claim to fame, and this is marginal fame at best, is that in the American circles, I coined a phrase that succinctly and accurately described what romantic encounters with Ukrainian/Russian girls was like. I call it "alligator wrestling." Trust me, I'm not exaggerating. Included in the package, you have all of the perks of alligator wrestling: drama, excitement, sweat, pain, extreme calorie burning and aerobic activity. All of these pleasures without the actual chance of being eaten. So, if you are the type of guy who likes the sweet*

*I shall leave any more details to your imagination. The one thing I can tell you for sure is that if you decide to visit a country like the Ukraine and date the women, you'd better take you're "A" game. I trained for an entire year in anticipation of great physical exertion (because Ukrainians walk for miles and miles and miles for the fun of it, too) and I still lost twenty pounds in two weeks in the Ukraine. Please do not do anything that perpetuates the stereotype of the lazy, fat American. We get a bad enough rap as it is from the Frenchmen who whisper behind our backs.*

# Chapter Five

## James Dean Lives!

*Although I am loathe to talk about the Ukrainian men, I realize I would be seriously remiss in my duties as a neutral observer if I did not comment on them.*

### Me Tarzan, you Jane

*They are sort of enigmatic.*

*They are not easy to explain. While it has been said by wiser people than me, the most fascinating thing about men is our utter simplicity, I'm not so sure Ukrainian men are as simple to categorize. They are not open-minded or easy-to-approach. They are guarded and very machoistic. A lot of James Dean wanabees; but I don't mean that in a bad way. They prefer black shirts, jeans, and James Dean's rebel attitude. Unless, of course, they're drunk. Then they become quite animated and charming. Don't we all? Which, luckily for me, is most of the time. So, there were some insights to be gleaned and revealed from the interactions with the Ukrainian men, without actually claiming that I understand them. They are definitely repressed by cultural dictates. Ukrainian men don't cry in public, ever. This repression of emotion plays at least some role in their shorter life expectancy, how much, could be debated by the mental health experts.*

## Why buy the cow, when you get the milk for free?

*The first mystery is the most obvious and the one everyone wants answered. If in fact, as I have already stated, that people are essentially the same everywhere, then why don't Ukrainian men get married at more or less the same rate as men in other civilized societies? Well, some of them do get married (there is a relatively small, but emerging middle class society springing up in the Ukraine), however, it's also true that most of them do not.*

## We have a lovely three bedroom cardboard ranch house within walking distance of a public toilet, and a heating grate

*Think of it in terms of American men. To understand the problem, personalize it. If you took the percentage of jobless American men and jobless Ukrainian men who are unmarried, it wouldn't be significantly different. A man's self worth is tied to two things: if he can maintain a job and if women (notably pretty women) like him. As Oscar Wilde once said, "you always make love to a pretty woman, and if she is plain, you make love to someone else". It is not exclusively an economic issue but economics is a major contributing factor. Look, even in families where there is plenty of money to go around, couples still fight. The two biggies (sources of greatest conflict) are sex and money. Well, I can't imagine sex being a problem area for Ukrainian* couples. However, the economic issue is legion. If a man is not able to hold down a good job, every little thing that goes wrong in the marriage will be magnified.

The same thing occurs in America.

### Rich man, poor man

Psychologists will tell you that the number one indicator of success in middle class marriages in America is if both sides are perceived as pulling their economic weight.

Sad, to be sure, but nonetheless true. However, in a bit of a statistical oddity, successful marriages in the lower economic class have no such correlation. So, if you want to hold onto a girl in America, you need to either make a significant amount of a money or troll your bait in trailer parks.

The economic issue, then, makes successful marriages an almost untenable proposition in the Ukraine. Successful marriages are still the exception, not the rule. Trust me, successful marriages in the Ukraine are not the same as successful marriages in America. In the Ukraine, if your husband only has two mistresses, that's a successful marriage. Guys, the only way you get a gig like that in America, is if you are ridiculously wealthy.

Of course there will always be that small percentage of women who marry only for love (trailer park queens) and don't care if their beloved has a job or not, but that percentage of women is smaller than the line of girls waiting to date Rush Limbaugh.

### Ladies, I think you're going to need a bigger broom

*Women want heroes. Men want damsels in distress. One hundred thousand years of sociological and anthropological evolutionary changes are not going to be brushed aside by thirty years of feminism.*

*You can ride that horse as long as you want, ladies, it won't ever make it out of the pasture.*

*Therein lies the problem.*

*Another fact, regardless of nationality, either from affluent societies like America or destitute societies like the Ukraine, damsels will eventually want babies. And they would prefer it if a husband was around to chip in. Being a hero is a tough gig no matter how good you are, but it becomes increasingly difficult if you don't have a job. Alas, men willingly volunteer for the first part of the task, the production end, but sadly, not the quality control and maintenance end. So, the end result is that you have hundreds of thousands, maybe millions of women with babies, who want husbands.*

### Batter up!

*Someone who is willing to step to the plate and take responsibility. Enter divorced and slightly aging single European and American men, (who young, vivacious, busty women in their own countries don't even know exist) who happen to think it's a pretty nice tradeoff.*

### *Anna Kournikova? Roseanne Arnold?*
### *Anna Kournikova? Roseanne Arnold?*
### *I can't decide. Leave me alone!*

*Seriously, ask yourself this. If you were a bald, slightly overweight middle-aged man (like a lot of Americans are) and you could marry someone like Anna Kournikova, maybe even significantly better, would you mind having a baby with her? By the way that was an obviously rhetorical question. No one could ever be so stupid they would miss that question. They say every day of the year, planes takes off from Russia or the Ukraine with hundreds of girls leaving their countries for greener pastures in search of husbands. In ten years, it will be thousands of girls a day, guaranteed. Count on it! Almost everyone you talk to in America knows of a man who has married a Russian woman. American men are not marrying foreign women for their accents. In a couple of hundred years in America there will be more children of a mixed American and Russian heritage than all others combined.*

*I will try and be frank with you, but you must know that I am no different from any of you. My life is what it is, I carry my own personal looking glass in which everything is measured and evaluated. I have had a beautiful life; I have beautiful kids and a beautiful future. I am not a bitter man.*

*I wouldn't be surprised if that was your first thought. I have no reason to be sour. Whether you believe me or not, I don't care.*

## Paradise lost and found

*Maybe some of my perceptions are off or askew or ever-so-slightly colored outside of the lines by my prejudiced (not racial, the kind of prejudice you get from seeing so much in life and deciding for yourself what you are willing to accept and not accept) eyes. I freely admit that. So, I am telling you that my interpretations and descriptions of the Ukraine and its people are the very best I could come up with, while acknowledging (as I did earlier in the book), that I have a filtering system to. I want to see everything. I want to know everything. However, I sadly realize that it is an unattainable goal.*

## We're gonna' need a bigger shovel

*Let's delve deeper into the Ukraine, shall we? We're discussing the men for now, so let's continue. There are lots of reasons why the Ukraine is a dangerous place to visit or live. First, while it is not a strange land, in say the way living in the Amazonian jungle with cannibals or Tibet with monks or bushmen in the African savannah is, or some other exotic or extreme existence. It is a different culture. I can't say it any louder than that. Pay close attention. The most likely way you will become extinct is through the public transportation system. The streets are narrow, uneven, and rough. Very rough. Some of the smaller cabs even disappear into some potholes temporarily, until they emerge on the other side. Big potholes. No, I'm not exaggerating, either. I'm sure you're wondering how they keep tires on the wheels then? I don't have the foggiest idea unless Ukrainian rubber is just tougher than ours or the tires are solid. Speaking of the transportation system, I will tell you that the other likely way to die is by the trains. Ok, I'm sure your mother taught you how to look both ways before crossing a street or in front of a speeding train, but these trains are different. There is very little safe space around these trains, and your reaction time is compressed, too. Also, from a practical standpoint, because of the winding nature of the streets and how the trains navigate in and around these streets, it is not only probable, but likely you will find yourself between a train and a building, with inches to spare many times. I was only almost killed twice, and I really was trying hard not to get myself killed.*

### A Kodak moment?

*Also, you get accosted, (a couple of young adult men took exception to me taking pictures of their square, and I already had images in the camera of someone I was rather fond of, so the only way they were going to extract that camera from my death grip was to pry my cold, dead fingers from around it) if you make a wrong move. In hindsight, this incident was considered by most American observers to be a most unusual and almost completely isolated incident. The odds of this kind of occurrence happening to an American were equated to the likelihood an airplane would fall out of the sky onto your head.*

### Almost famous

*I could just imagine how the headlines the next day in the Dnepropetrovsk Daily News might read, "Stupid American tourist dies to save picture of Ukrainian girlfriend; what an idiot." I managed to convince them that I was indeed a tourist and not an American spy, so they slinked off, but they definitely were spoiling for a fight. Don't expect the police to rapidly come to your aid. You are, after all (and while few Ukrainians would verbalize this remark, I'm pretty sure they don't care if you get yourself killed by thieves or Gypsies), a foreigner in their country with possibly sinister motives.*

### They shoot Gypsies, don't they?

*Oh yes, the Gypsies. Most European countries have bands of Gypsies roaming the streets. Well, not roaming actually, but they're around. I believe slinking is their preferred mode of travel. Whether justified or not, I can't say, but they are a hated people. I was involved in another serious incident that included a Gypsy. I got in very late one night and I was just hanging around on the square sitting on the fountain drinking some cold drinks and minding my own business.*

### Of all the Gin joints and fountains in the world, you had to sit by me

*I noticed that an unusual looking woman in tattered clothes came and sat beside me. If you had to imagine what a Gypsy might look like, she would probably come close. What stood out to me, besides her street person apparel, were her eyes. They were black, cold, lifeless eyes. You couldn't possibly look into her eyes for very long without being adversely affected. It was just a very unnerving experience like none I had ever had before.*

## Kid, how'd you like to go for a swim at the bottom of the fountain?

*Suddenly, a little Ukrainian boy walked up to us and started throwing things on her and breaking bottles at her feet. Being a fairly chivalrous American, I wasn't going to let some little Ukrainian punk abuse a woman. I told him to stop; he didn't. I chased him off and he came back. He was persistent, so was I. He grew weary of my rantings and ran off. I didn't notice anything unusual until a fellow American walked up to me and said that all the locals were staring at me. I explained to him what had just transpired. He took one look at the girl and started laughing. He told me I had defended the honor of a Gypsy woman and that I should never do that again. A major cultural faux-paus, and another way to get yourself dead, without even know why you got yourself dead.*

## For the love of God, someone give them Cher's address

*They commonly kill Gypsies in Western European countries because of their supposed treachery such as stealing babies, robbing people, and hanging out on village fountains. He said I was lucky I wasn't attacked by the locals seeking to vindicate their adolescent brethren.*

*Also, another incident to show the possibly dangerous existence of a foreigner. At one point while riding in a cab in the remote part of the city at night, while stopped at a light, we were rushed by two thugs from the brush. The cab driver spotted them and took off just before they got to my door. Who knows what their intentions were? Kill me, rob me, or maybe to just welcome me to the Ukraine. I don't really know.*

## Barney Fifeskys

*I never actually saw police cars in motion while I was there. Of the few police cars I did see, the officers were just sitting around in the parks and talking to each other. So, it's rpetty much frontier-style law or non-existent law enforcement. Which brings me to one of my essential tenents about the Ukraine being dangerous. A woman friend confided to me (because I was curious) that of all the things that holds her country back and keeps their economy suppressed, the worst is the lack of commonly upheld laws. She claimed there was too much corruption on many different levels. She waved her hand like a snake and said, "very crooked, everything." Again, sort of like a frontier ecosystem. The local land baron owned the local sheriff who protected the local establishments from the bad guys, for a price.*

## More agents than you can shake a small stick at

*The mobsters, corrupt politicians, ex-KGB agents, and Ukrainian security agents, have the only cushy jobs in the country, like managing the prostitutes and building projects. So, there is definitely danger lurking in the shadows if you cross the wrong people.*

## **Unless your name is Robin Williams, I wouldn't crack too many jokes**

*Ukrainian men might find your careless silly, comedic, casual behavior amusing (or at least the few who understand English will) if they are drunk, but don't count on wowing the locals with that behavior if they are sober. Ukrainians don't like casual language and loose mannerisms. Ukranian men like precise words and logical rational thoughts-very no nonsense. A Ukrainian friend put it to me like this. Americans say okay way too much. Life is either good, or it's bad, it is never okay. In their experiences this is absolutely true. Very seldom is a Ukrainian's life ever just okay. Try to remember this if you can. The word I've been looking for is standoffish. And it's a good description of at least the Ukrainian men. However, I've been told that is due more to the language barrier than it is with a bad attitude. I don't exactly go out of my way in America to engage foreign nationals either, do you?*

*Look, they don't have a lot of reasons to be cheery. It's cold in the winter, bone chilling cold, and it's like a Minnesota winter, not a Florida or a California winter. Their weather even induces melancholy. From a merely physiological, scientific standpoint, they don't receive enough sunlight to trigger the biochemical reactions that release the happy hormones. How would you like to stay inside three or four months freezing your tail off, waiting for the sun to come back out. And maybe not even have hot water for your shower, in the winter!!! Because of their northern longitude, they have a lot of daylight in the summer, so guess what they have a lot of in the winter? Dark, very good. So they already have a built in reason to be pissed off at the world from the get go. They don't have very good jobs, if they have a job at all. Maybe in a factory, maybe driving a cab, it's not going to be a good job. And they have a short life expectancy to top everything else off, due to their lifestyle.*

*Why do they have a short life expectancy? This is another important part, so pay attention.*

## Bridge over troubled water

*In a word, the Ukraine, Russia and other CIS states sponsor alcoholism to fight dissidence. They have to. With the bleak existence they have, you've got to throw them a bone somewhere. The population can buy alcohol cheaper than they can eat a meal. State-sponsored alcoholism is a bridge between civil unrest and a contented population. If they can't get the people to cross over that bridge, the government is going to be in deep doo-doo. Unhappy masses tend to riot in the streets until someone figures out a way to get them happy. Which in fact the Ukrainians just did. They rioted in the streets because of the last crooked presidential election. Americans do the same thing to a lesser degree. Generally speaking, alcohol is the last legal drug that keeps several strata of our populace happy. The poor and downtrodden, homeless, rednecks, and the wealthy. Did I leave anyone out? Oh, yeah, the middle class, sorry. We tried prohibition and while most people in America don't believe it worked, these people in fact get the history wrong, it did work. The vast majority of Americans stopped drinking because there just wasn't ready access to alcohol outside of moonshiners and those in big cities. However, bootleggers (not the government) got very rich off the common people and crime and criminal activity associated with the production of illegal alcohol soared to new heights.*

## Trickle-down economics versus voodoo economics

If the economics of the Ukraine ever improved, alcoholism would be all but eliminated. The only way they will ever have a vibrant economy is by switching from socialistic tendencies in the business world to a free market economic system.

Which the Ukrainians are of course in the process of doing as I write. They need free market principles to be applied to their dire economic realities. They must have more competition in the business sector, access to capital for working class Ukrainians, and financial incentives to more of the private sector workers. I could be wrong, but I think a working class girl at a McDonald's, doesn't make a lot less money than a woman doctor there. I know of one girl who was a nurse, and they had an economic crisis in the country (several banks failed, and I'm pretty sure they didn't have FDIC insurance for investors to recoup their money), and she wasn't paid for six months.

But . . . she still had to go to work.

Do you think you would go to work if your boss told you they weren't going to pay you for six months? But socialism is deeply rooted in the nationalism and the culture of the people. They want to change to a free market economic system about as much as we want to become a socialistic system. They know it isn't good for them, however. I mean if you were starving to death in a run-down flat and you knew in your heart that you were a dedicated and hard worker, I'll bet you could figure out for yourself that there was something rotten in Dnepropetrovsk.

Additional problems that arise in the Ukraine are that sometimes a phone cable will be broken in a flat complex, and *because of the plodding, sometimes inefficient government, services may not be restored for a month.*

*The same types of mishaps occur with the hot water supply and electricity.*

*You may also need to see a doctor, but you may not be able to get in right away. There are lots of people in the Ukraine who have obvious medical conditions, like terrible skin cancers or infirmities of old age that go untreated. Some of the women are almost completely bent over. When they are walking down the sidewalks they are looking at their shoes.*

*The government is inconsistent (it is possible to live in a flat and pay no bills for months and not get evicted) and obviously susceptible to bribes and corrupt behavior reminiscent of Chicago under Daly's regime or Tammany Hall in New York, in the thirties. On the other hand, they keep meticulous records of things like how many times your children get treated at the hospital, which they will use against you if they need to: for instance, if you decide to immigrate.*

*There is a feeling of quiet desperation that exists here.*

*The American correlation would be the early thirties after the Great Depression hit. People really wanted to work, but there wasn't any work to be had.*

*Ukrainians know that things are not going to change anytime soon. It's actually complicated. They are a universally hardworking, bright people living in a country with great natural resources, but they just don't have the economic wherewithal to do the things they have to do. Additionally, the local highly corrupt bureaucrats siphon off almost all of the countries wealth. If this money were put back into the places it belonged, (instead of their pockets) like infrastructure, health care, and public assistance: the Ukraine would be close to Utopia.*

*They should have the same type of infrastructure that America has. They should have the same standard of living that America has. As I've mentioned before, their socialistic tendencies from the past keep them economically repressed. The old Soviet Union was obviously isolationistic, that didn't help. They also have brutal winters (except in the south) that affect the production and transportation of goods and services in the same way as in America (or any country where the roads are sometimes impassable) or at least painstakingly slow.*

*It really comes down to one simple economic reality. You can't make money without spending money. How do you think Donald Trump got rich? Someone loaned him some startup money, (his dad) and his genius did the rest. But, even Donald Trump had help getting started.*

*Someone (in either European or American banks) has to be willing to invest billions of dollars in your country (retooling factories, subsidizing the farmers who sometimes starve by the millions,) and modernizing the rest of the nation's transportation and infrastructure, (roads and bridges). Or, corporations like General Motors, Coke, or IBM have to come aboard, or more to the point, come abroad. Why would any of these companies want to take a gamble this large in an unproven/unestablished economic arena?*

*These are just some of the issues that come up. Am I trying to deter you from visiting the Ukraine or Russia? Absolutely not.*

*I believe it's as close to Heaven as you will get on earth.*

## *If your last name is Yushchenko, you might want to stay away from the Borsch*

*Are you in more danger in the Ukraine than you are in America? Probably, but maybe no more so than you would be in any country where your language skills and unfamiliarity with the customs would get you killed. Even in my hometown of Big Spring (which is a very small town in Texas) back in the States, there were places I wouldn't go after dark.*

## *Since Russia is still poisoning their enemies, I wonder if Putkin got the memo about the Cold War being over?*

*I will tell you that your best strategy is to maintain as low a profile as you possibly can. The Ukraine is not a country where you want to engage in your typical animated, conspicuous behavior. Be sure to overindulge and over complement and be overly gracious when you are dealing with Ukrainian citizens.*

# Chapter Six

## What your mother never told you about girls like Olga

*So when do we get to the good stuff? I'm working on it. I will start things off with a cautionary tale for your reading pleasure. A good laugh will be had at my expense.*

### At least my pickup lines have a puncher's chance of working now

First, some background information. In Dnepropetrovsk, like all the other major Ukrainian and Russian cities, there are agencies that focus on shall we say, international dating. Let's face it, about ninety-five percent of the Ukrainian citizens don't speak English, so either you spend countless hours trying to wade haphazardly through the streets hoping to meet someone who either may or may not want to go out with you.

Which will be hard to ascertain if they don't speak English (one young lad I know of, spent hours trying to ask out a shop girl) or you find help. I happened to use "A Foreign Affair" dating agency for my intial in road into the Ukraine, and found everyone in the agency, from the consultants at the *top, to the people employed "in country" (where the agencies are that house the catalogues of available women for your perusal)assisting all of these wandering "lost" Americans, to be very professional, caring, and accomadating with every request.*

*It's actually quite logical if you look at it from the right context. First, while most of the single men who visit the Ukraine are at least curious about the culture (the Ukraine stands alone on its own merits. There is history to be studied around every corner and every museum. There are opera houses and sports halls, magnificently maintained parks, gourmet food, daily craft fairs and many other cultural attractions too numerous to list here), the women, however, are the mightiest curiosity. Dating agencies may seem too arranged for your delicate sensibilities. They put you of a mind of an escort service. But they give you indispensable valuable biographical data such as age, interests, hobbies, and children which can help you separate out potential girlfriends from the herd. In America, you typically have to date a girl several times to gather information that will rule her either in or out as a potential mate. You end up wasting not only a bunch of your time, but hers, too. The agencies save you from lots of needless dates with girls you wouldn't possibly want to ever be with. I will talk about this in depth later. If you saved up the money you spent dating American girls for one year, you could stay in the Ukraine for months.*

## Survey says

*Probably the most commonly asked question I get from American men is how many of the girls are serious about coming to America, as opposed to just being curious about foreign men and wanting to get some free dinners and dancing? And how would a civilian (American) know the difference. Tough question. I don't think there is any way to accurately or truthfully answer that question. Who would keep these kinds of statistics, anyway? I could take a guess, but that's all it would be. Even if you had all of the girls in the Ukraine fill out a survey, it would be worthless paper. There are always going to be girls that say they love their country and would never leave it, but then they might meet someone who convinces them otherwise. A woman who falls in love with a man will probably follow him anywhere, even America. Or it could happen in reverse. A woman who is dead set on leaving the Ukraine, after being exposed to base American men, might decide that things in her country aren't so bad after all.*

### Back to the future

*Back to my point. I was walking around Dnepropetrovsk with Lance one day, and we walked into a dating agency. I was thumbing through the pages, and one girl in particular caught my eye. She caught my eye because she looked like Anna Kournikova. Five minutes later they called her, and I had a date for that evening.*

*Boy, was I excited.*

*Tom and Anna Kournikova going on a date*

*Welcome to the big time, Miss Kournikova.*

*This girl just got the call up from the minors to the bigs. The future Mrs. Tom Posey was some kind of looker. I didn't know who was luckier, me or her.*

## The worm turns

*Lance was excited for me, too. He couldn't believe my good fortune. I spent a couple of hours getting myself as handsome as possible considering my age and state of deterioration.*

*The witching hour had struck.*

## Dead man walking

*I was headed down the stairs to meet Olga in the lobby and was met by Lance who was on the second floor landing area.*

*He had a look on his face somewhere between sheer horror and abject grief. It was the look of a man who had stared death, square in the eye, and recently, too. If you could have only seen the look on his face you would have been scared to, very scared.*

*He managed to squeak out the words. "Tom, it isn't good. I wouldn't go down there if I were you. She looks like Brett Favre. Which in hindsight confused me a little bit.*

*Brett Favre is, after all, a nice looking man, but if he were a woman, I'm not sure this woman would be so pretty. I had to quickly do the gender transformation in my head, and I just couldn't quite imagine what she was going to look like. I'm a lot of things that aren't good: impertinent, impatient, impudent, and a lot of other "im" words. I willingly acknowledge that. But my daddy taught me to always be a gentleman. How could I ever complain about a woman standing me up if I engaged in the same kind of behavior?*

## Don't call me, I'll call you

*If she looks like Brett Favre that much, maybe she just resembles a good ole solid corn fed girl. Who among us doesn't like to date a corn-fed girl ever now and again?*

*Of course I'll go down the stairs. How bad could it be?*

*I shouldn't have.*

*I really should have faked my own death, or at least a heart attack. Or just sprinted back up the stairs and barricaded myself in my room. No, that's not going to work. I didn't have enough furniture to pile against the door to resist her charge.*

*Hell, even jumping out of my four story window was a better option than the one I chose.*

*Suffice it to say, she didn't look like Anna Kournikova! Well, maybe if Anna Kournikova had swallowed two adults, and got hit in the face repeatedly with a blunt instrument*

*She was brutally ugly.*

*And she was much too large to back out on. I'm a big boy, but she could have whipped my ass with one blow of her mammoth fists. She resembled nothing so much as a hippopotamus with a backpack.*

*I still managed to pull off some decorum and quickly asked her what she wanted to do, although I already knew her answer was going to involve food.*

*So, let's begin this modern day tale of Beauty and the Beast. For factual purposes of storytelling, I will be playing the part of the Beauty, Olga, the Beast.*

### *Borsch, it's not just for breakfast anymore*

*We walked about a block and ducked inside a mall for some borsch and Turkish bread. Boy, she could eat. I kept my fingers and other essential body parts a safe distance away from her frenetic feeding frenzy. A pack of starving hyenas are less ravenous than Olga. Watching her eat actually made me nervous. I was thinking a romantic interlude with Olga would have been a death-defying stunt Evil Kneivel would have even balked at. I mean there's your garden variety foolish behavior, jumping over dozens of vehicles on a motorcycle, then there's your "I really want to die this time" behavior.*

### *Is there a priest in the house available to administer last rites?*

*Sex with Olga . . .*
*Of course I had already figured out there was going to be an immediate scam in my future, I just didn't know what the nature of the scam would be.*
*It only took a few minutes before I knew.*
*Olga (surprise, surprise) was in the mood to shop.*

### *Stepford Russian sales chicks*

*When we walked into an exclusive women's wear store, those perfectly built porcelain doll sales ladies looked at me as if I had Roseanne Arnold's ugly fat sister in tow. They were paralyzed. None of them dared render aid.*

## Undoubtedly, the second indignity in life or death, this poor mink had to endure

*Olga grabbed (I'm not kidding) the most expensive mink stole I have ever seen in my life and tried it on. Oh God, please don't let it tear!!! I believe the price was like ninety thousand grivnas. Around three thousand dollars! She asked me how she looked, I lied and told her marvelous, but unbelievably, I didn't bring ninety thousand grivnas with me. So I don't think I can buy it for you today. I told her I felt terrible and apologized for not robbing a bank before we came in the mall to shop.*

*Now, I know what you are going to say. And you are going to be right. "Tom, you are an idiot." It's just that at the time, I was a little scared of her, and I was caught a little bit off guard by her aggressive behavior. I'm usually a true gentlemen, and gentlemen don't insult ladies. Well, I know she wasn't technically a lady, but I'm just not a mean person.*

## Russian charades don't really suit me

*This charade continued in every store we went in, about fifteen or twenty stores. She would pick something out, and I would say it looks wonderful, but I steadfastly told her "no" each time.*

*Now, there was a method to her madness. Olga was testing the water. She was trying to find out just how much money I would spend to get rid of her. She had probably scammed dozens, if not hundreds of unsuspecting stupid Americans with the same basic strategy.*

*She started out with the mink stole and ever so gradually reduced the price of the things she was asking for.*

## Where's Omar the tentmaker, when you need him?

*In one of the last stores we visited, she had finally became exasperated with me rebuffing her requests, and she said "Tom, I do not care what you buy me, I just want you to pick out something you think would look good on me." I wanted to say, "Well, anything that will cover you from head to toe and is opaque, is going to be good for me," but, alas, I said there wasn't anything in this store that I liked.*

*After about two or three hours (I know, I know, I was a special kind of idiot for not showing her the door after I determined she was scamming me), we arrived at the last store.*

*She picked out a doll of some kind that attached to her backpack. She said, "Tom, you will buy me this pretty lady, I must have her, Tom." Well, I should have bought it for her. It was only thirty two grivnas, but I was already worked up and mad by this point in the date. I told her "no", and that I needed to go back and find my friend. She began to make a big scene and wag the doll in my face and hit my chest with it. I guess this was her last tactic.*

## I was envisioning a choke hold in my immediate future

*The strong-arm maneuver.*
*She was drawing a crowd.*

*It was getting uglier and uglier. She gave me one last look, almost imploring me to buy it for her. I shook my head no, and she finally pivoted on her massive foot and quickly darted out of the store, never to be seen or heard from again. Well, not by me, anyway. She probably had more dates lined up that evening with more unsuspecting fools.*

## I can't feel my legs

*I had entered the early stages of shock immediately following the date with Olga (slightly traumatized and victimized) and felt an overwhelming urge to sleep. My body's self defense mechanism had gone into motion to try and save itself.*

## Karmic payback for long ago slights against girls?

*It took me a whole day to recover from my date with Olga. Everywhere I walked, I expected to see Olga coming around the next corner. I imagined her to be waiting to jump out from behind a tree or a monument (as if they could conceal her presence), to launch a surprise attack against me, to gain her revenge against me for not buying her the mink stole, or at least the pretty lady backpack doll.*

*I eventually recovered my nerve and finally got a grip on myself.*

*It was surely one of the most disquieting moments in my life, but it's things like the date with Olga, that reveal your true nature. The important thing was not that I allowed myself to be scammed or tricked into a date with a hideously deformed hippopotamus. The important thing was how I responded to adversity. I think I did okay. I even took a mild beating from the pretty lady backpack attachment doll in stride.*

*Olga didn't arrive at this point in her life overnight. Overweight, hostile, and deceitful, Olga had some setbacks along the way. Who knows what mistreatment or misfortune she'd had to endure? There but for the grace of God, go all of us. Those of us who have led charmed lives (loving parents, good friends, economic advantages) would do well to keep these things in mind when interacting with people less fortunate than ourselves.*

# Chapter Seven

## Jenny Craig My Ass

*The next liaison I had would be infinitely more pleasurable. I had been told by an interpreter about a young teacher who was a very special lady.*

*Her name was Elena. I agreed to meet her for lunch.*

*She took a cab down to my hotel to meet me.*

*I waited in the lobby for her to appear.*

### Weird science

While I'm on the subject of dating, I will take a brief respite to tell you about another important distinction between Ukrainian girls and American girls. Being a man of science and a man of romantic intentions, I thought I would try a little experiment. My friends and I have often lamented the fact that in America if you ask a girl out, there is no better than a fifty-fifty chance she will actually go out with you. American girls have a scurrilous reputation for backing out of dates at the last minute.

### Husband training 101

*I don't know why. It's probably a tactic that mothers teach their daughters. It's their way of finding out how much crap a man will take, or if he's willing to put up with treacherous behavior to secure your affections. I suppose they figure that if a man is willing to be treated badly from the outset of the relationship, he probably makes good husband material.*

### Oh, what a tangled web we weave

*With this in mind, I asked two American girls out for the same night. I was going to check out my hypothesis. If my hypothesis was correct, at least one of them would be a no-show. If I was wrong, I was going to have to own up to being a jerk.*

*What a nice social commentary this would prove to be for my book.*

*Unbelievably, or not, they both canceled.*

### I'll bet Einstein didn't have this much trouble with women

*I went to a favorite guru, friend, and asked him for a conclusive observation on what he thought about my experimental results. He offered the following observation. "Well, Tom, I guess you're thrilled that you've discovered a completely heretofore unknown scientific principle tonight." A conundrum for the ages. I did? Really, what would that be, oh, wise guru? Easy, he tells me. "How many American*

*girls does a man have to ask out to actually have a date?"*
*Apparently, it will always be one more than he actually asks.*

## Bandades anyone?

*Ouch! And I mean ouch for you American girls out*
*there? That's just a scathing indictment and truism waiting*
*to become part of the American lexicon. And you seriously*
*wonder why thousands of men fly to the end of the world to*
*date women?*
*Right!*
*In my realm of scientific observation and investigation,*
*I have concluded that Ukrainian women don't stand up men*
*with dates. Now, they might not go out with you, which is*
*fine, but if they like you enough to accept a date with you,*
*they will not back out. Refreshing.*
*Now, for the date with Elena.*
*She stepped out of the taxi right on schedule. Elena*
*looked like the proverbial girl next door. Well, only if you*
*lived in Dnepropetrovsk would she look like the girl next*
*door. Her hair was the color of honey. She was extremely*
*shapely, and had the brightest blue eyes I have ever seen in*
*my life.*
*From the moment I first introduced myself, I was*
*captivated by her.*

## I'll take one gob of sugar please

*She had that singular universal quality that all*
*elementary teachers (even in the Ukraine I suppose) have in*
*spades. She oozed sweetness.*

*We walked to her favorite park and sat and talked for several hours. Actually I did the talking, she did the listening.*

### The only known naturally occurring vacuum on Earth, is between a man's ears

*I will admit that it is hard for men (because we don't have the best radar system in the world, obviously) to know for sure with any woman if they're genuinely interested in you, or if they have some kind of hidden agenda or ulterior motive that gives them the ability to feign interest in you. Obviously, when you are talking about the male ego, a man will usually think all women of every age, size, and shape are interested in him, so that's a hell of a filtering system. "I don't know for sure, Bubba, but she couldn't take her eyes off of me. I think I was mesmerizing her." Yeah, she was mesmerized alright; she was mesmerized by something. Maybe it was your insensitivity or stupidity, or the fact that you couldn't tell the salad fork from the soup spoon at dinner, or other sundry social inadequacies, or it could have been your self-centered ramblings and pomposity. Who knows? With most men there is a whole plethora of common attributes to mesmerize women.*

*Ukrainian women do have additional motivation to string you along. Some women will do that. Just like a woman in America or any other country will. America is a much wealthier country than the one they live in. It's much warmer for sure, well, except for Minnesota. All Ukrainians are aware of the fact that America is the land of opportunity. It surely is, too. Almost any Ukrainian girl can set foot on American soil and be considered a wealthy woman. But will*

they have a real life in America compared to the Ukraine;
probably not in their minds?

If Elena had lived in America instead of the Ukraine,
she had the potential to be a movie star. She was a looker.

### Get em'right after they've been potty-trained

Strangely enough, it wasn't even her physical beauty
that was her best feature. She was engaging to talk to (perfect
English, much better than mine) and alternately charming,
exuberant and refined. Very fascinating. But very young.

Elena was a welcome respite from the malevolent
Olga. Ooh.

I knew from the start that Elena was no scam artist. She
was genuine. She listened to me intently. I had her full, rapt
attention. I was able to hold her spellbound with many tales
of American life, and I gave her repeated servings of various
slices of Americana.

### Can I get an amen?

Once again, I was preaching to the converts though.
Two of Elena's best friends had already married in the last
two years and went to America ahead of her.

One of them had gone to Chicago, the other to Iowa.
Her friends had written her many letters and regaled her
with tales of America as the land of milk and honey. They
lied. Elena was ready to make her own move. Or at least,
that's the gist of what I gathered by talking to her. My first
clue was that while I'm a pretty good orator, I usually need a
captive subject in order to hold someone spellbound.

Not Elena, she hung on my every word, with bated breath. You would have thought I had a direct uplink to God, and He was spilling the secret to life to me one syllable at a time. She never stopped looking into my eyes. After what seemed like hours of orating, our posteriors grew sore, so we went for a stroll back toward the main square.

## Dejavu all over again

We went in to the same mall that Olga and I had the great misfortune to patronize from the previous day. Talk about a Nam flashback!

We sat at a small café and sipped ice tea.

She refused to eat so much as an appetizer.

I persisted, but so did she.

I would discover in due time, why she wouldn't break bread with me.

I really wanted her to eat something, because I was hungry (which is about to be real important information), but she wouldn't budge.

## Anorexia nervosa seemed to be more likely

The reason why Elena wouldn't eat was about to emerge. Don't worry, it's nothing sinister, it's just revelatory.

When at last we finished our tea, I asked Elena what she wanted to do next. She wanted to go for another walk. Fair enough. Almost all dates with Ukrainians at least start out with a walk or end with a walk. Or you have a walk in between your walks. I had a more sedentary activity in mind for Elena and myself, but, hey, it was a lovely day for a stroll.

### Comfortable shoes, the true secret of happiness when you get over forty

*But this was not to be your run-of-the-mill meandering-let's-hang-out-in-the-park and sit and talk kind of walk.*

### Marathon man

*We took off towards the Dnepr River, which was several miles from the mall. Ok, a healthy walk I told myself, but very doable. I am after all a physical specimen. We then proceeded down stream several more miles to a famous park (now we're ranging a little bit) that had amusement rides and a bridge and then back up Karl Marx Avenue (Hey! The Battan Death March was shorter than this) to the place we had started. It was a walk of no less than five or six miles. Over hill and dale, too. And Elena did it in heels!*

*Now, just like the date with Olga, I didn't complain. I knew there must be a higher power at work. In the case of Olga, I knew that I was learning how to persevere under a cruel tyrant and a horribly mean-spirited person. With Elena, it was the thrill of victory and the agony of defeat rolled up into one package.*

### Guys are so pathetic

*My legs were about to fall off (definitely the down side), but, dang it, (the up side) she sure did look good on my arm.*

*I don't honestly remember at what point Elena told me why we were on a walking safari (probably because my* brain was oxygen-deprived), but the real reason was, well, astounding.

First things first.

## Joan Crawford was a piker

*Ukrainian girls love their mothers. They are close, close, close. They love them like Roseanne loves fudge brownies. They can be seen walking arm and arm down city streets. It really is cute. They have the same kind of reverence for their mothers that the Asians have for their elders. They also tell them all of the gruesome details of their dating adventures. No details are left to the imagination, which is certainly a different approach than American mothers and daughters have. If you question them on this subject, they will tell you, "Of course I tell my mother everything, don't you?" They are more like girlfriends to them, than mothers. If their mothers tell them something, they, by God, listen.*

*The reason we walked so far will help to illuminate one of the major cultural differences between America and the Ukraine.*

## Now for an alternate viewpoint

*Elena explained to me that earlier in the day, her mother had sat her down for a talk.*

*Her mother had admonished her to start exercising more because she was getting fat. Good lord, she looked like a swimsuit model. Her mother told her to not come back home until she had walked all night. Which probably meant all evening, but, still, she was perfect. The weight issue is something that the Ukrainians are conscious about.*

## *Obesity the last great plague*

*The last statistic I read in America had from thirty to sixty percent (depending on socio-economic status) of American children as obese. And I mean actually obese, not swimsuit model obese like Elena. Some States have produced statistical evidence that suggests that there is a growing percentage of adolescents in America who are becoming uneducable due to their poor overall health. Most of these health related issues are correlated to the level of obesity in that state.*

*Schools have to implement special programs to address this issue. They must show documentation of tracking methods and corrective measures they use to aid the children. Fascinating. How about the obese kid's parents chasing their asses from the dinner table? Or how about putting a lock on the fridge? How's that for a program? Schools monitoring obese children? Who gave birth here? The schools?*

## *Americans have never met a potato chip they didn't like*

*A medical journal in America claims that obesity in the 21$^{st}$ century will kill more people (obesity is related to cancer, heart disease and diabetes) than all of the plagues combined in human history.*

*Elena was a fantastic girl. She would have made a perfect wife. She was certainly receptive to the idea of living in America. I would have treated her like a princess, too. She might have even brought me inexpressible joy.*

*Elena was a Monet painting. She was full of splendid color and expressiveness. Elena was a ravishing beauty. But like a Monet, she was better off observed from a far, than possessed. She deserved a grander fate than the one I could offer her. My conscience (while not always present, occasionally rears its ugly head) prevented me from pursuing Elena. Dammit!*

*She was just so young and so pretty; I couldn't help but feel sub-conscious around her. I mean I look good for an old guy, but I'm not twenty four anymore.*

### A younger non-fossilized version of myself

*I don't know if Elena will be able to find a young, handsome man in the Ukraine to marry her, the type of man that she obviously deserves to have.*

*Maybe, her life with me would have been much better than the life she would have in the Ukraine with a Ukrainian man. Maybe, that's where the tradeoff comes in to play for these girls. But, when something doesn't feel right, you have to listen to those feelings.*

### Some girls just like crust on their bread

*How many times in America had I noticed an aging fossil with a woman just like Elena and disparaged him as being a cradle robber? Too many times to count. They could very well have been madly in love, too. I didn't know.*

### I'm a part-time hypocrite; I don't have the time or energy to go full-time

Women are not as shallow as men when it comes to the age discrepancy. I'm not going to be a hypocrite; at least not about this I'm not.

### I had a lovely spot on the wall of my den all picked out, too

I let Elena off the hook. I almost had her on the bank, and then, inexplicably, I let her slip through my hands. I let her fall back into the vastness of the dark sea that is the Ukraine, possibly to oblivion, possibly even to a worse fate than having to live with a pompous old guy. I'll probably never know. My, she would have made a lovely trophy, too.

# Chapter Eight

## *A love letter to Marina*
### *(Part One)*

*Now for something completely different (as Monty Python was want to say), a special memory. Maybe, a once in a lifetime memory. Maybe not. I've learned to not make any bold pronouncements or predictions, and to absolutely never, say never. There is only one good way to begin the tale, at the beginning. This tale will necessitate that we eventually venture ever so briefly out of our native habitat, the Ukraine. But it is an essential trip. My tale may not be the definitive experience of everyman, or of what would necessarily happen to you, but it does have an element of the possible, of the probable attached to it.*

### Except at no time in my story will knives be used

*We are all unique individuals. People either have a special chemistry or they don't. Either they mesh together like your own hand in your favorite glove, or they fit like O.J. Simpson's glove supposedly did, not well. The story will serve as a useful primer on the exposition of cross-cultural relationship differences and also, to a lesser degree, as a* cautionary tale. But probably not in the way you think it will. In my visit to Dnepropetrovsk, I of course met many lovely women, and like I said before, the men were not all that communicative. So, I was basically forced to limit my communication to the women of the Ukraine.

What a tough break.

Enter Marina . . . For some unknown reason there is an unbelievable name shortage in the Ukraine. There are tens of millions of girls and only about twenty or thirty names. Strange, but not illogical, considering their mindset. They just choose to have the same practical economy of names as they actually have shortages of real goods in the real economy. Anyway, back to Marina.

### I just love typing Dnepropetrovsk

Our story begins in Dnepropetrovsk. I had spent the last week of my trip dating Marina in Dnepropetrovsk. I had dated other girls, but I hadn't felt like there was any sort of special connection. Which may also serve to debunk the myth that a man can just show up in Russia, grab the first beautiful girl he sees, propose marriage and live happily ever after. I absolutely, positively guarantee you that women all over the world are the same in this respect. They are emotional, tender creatures, one and all. If you aren't willing to carefully navigate that metaphorical stream to get to their heart, to the source of the fountain, forget it. Stay home and watch bass fishing in your boxers. Only a woman experiencing total frustration, forced to live in sheer destitution, would leave all of her family behind to go live in a country she doesn't understand, with a man she doesn't love. I can't speak for Ukrainian or Russian girls, but I think *they would tell you that freezing their asses off all winter and possibly dying from starvation is a much preferable fate than the one I just mentioned.*

*Marina worked out of the Hotel Central as an interpreter. Her job was to assist mostly American and European men who were dating girls who had limited English skills. She was an enchanting girl. She was unlike any girl I had ever met in my life. From the first time I saw her, I knew there was something different about her. She had a unique quality of just looking into your eyes with a kind of intensity I had never seen before. It's not like she was the first beautiful woman I have ever encountered in my life. But never before had I encountered a woman as unique as Marina. With her combination of mannerisms, the way she held herself, her imposing physical stature, her voice, and those brown eyes that pierced me like daggers in my heart, she just had a combination of attributes that were entirely her own. She was special, very special. Ukrainian women are not beautiful in an exotic sense like Asian or Hispanic women are. Their bone structure is more like ethnic Europeans, and Scandinavians. They have a more sensual allure. Marina, however, was not your typical Russian beauty. She possessed black hair and brown eyes. She had more of an Asian appearance than a Russian one.*

*She had started out her life in Russia, and then her parents immigrated to the Ukraine for employment possibilities when the Soviet Union collapsed. They died soon after they immigrated, under mysterious circumstances she did not care to elaborate on. Marina was raised by several of her uncles. I was obviously smitten by Marina early in the relationship.*

## Well, it's not going to do him any good now

*I soon found myself drawn to her offices where she would make me hot tea and I would make myself comfortable on a dilapidated sofa that Lenin probably had in an outer office a hundred years ago and just watch her as she worked the phones and conversed with the men who came in and out of the office. You should know that listening to a Russian girl speak English is very exciting.*

## Which certainly saves on hypnosis

*They can put you into a trance you may not be able to recover from if you aren't on your guard. I'm serious. Listening to a Russian girl speak English will get you intoxicated faster than swigging Russian vodka. I was a content fellow to sit for hours and just stare at her and listen to her talk. I tried to stay out of the way, so she didn't seem to mind.*

*Marina usually got off around 6:00pm and we would go out for dinner.*

*She lived several miles out of the city and it was more practical to stay in the city than to go back to her flat. It was the first week in June, the best time of the year to be in Dnepropetrovsk. Ukrainians suffer through an agonizing, perpetually long winter and a crisply cool spring to get to this moment in time.*

### Now, if we can just get them to stop doing even that, I will have something to write home about

*The summer months. They're not about to waste the glorious feeling of warmth on their skin by covering their bodies with clothes. This fact explains why the women dress, well . . . let's say skimpily, for lack of a better expression, during the summer months. Like an Englishman that goes mad in the midday sun, they revel in the heat, bask in the brilliant midday sun.*

*So, Marina and I would normally walk around for a couple of hours, usually in the many parks, while she gave me historical, cultural and social lessons on her country. I soaked it up like a sponge. She told me stories of their heroes and heroic battles, of the stories behind their breathtaking monuments, and of poets and politicians from long ago. She wove beautiful stories of the mythology and the folklore of Russian literary tales, all the time speaking in her somewhat chopped up English. Actually, her English wasn't much worse than a typical American high school student. On the up side, I felt drunk and deliriously happy when in her presence. I was enthralled by her charming mannerisms and extremely maternalistic, doting, protective behavior.*

### Oedipus, my Oedipus, wherefore art thou?

*Psychologists will tell you that all men are looking for a woman who on some level reminds them of their mother in some key way. It could even be on a subconscious level, but psychologists claim this maternalism is the sociology of what triggers men to like whom they like. Marina obviously had classic mothering tendencies. On the other hand, all*

*Ukrainian girls are like that. Maybe they are repressed by the lack of media images (unlike American women) and deep-rooted cultural factors, and more dependent on men to survive than other western societies. I can only speculate. Adult American women are just as independent as men; they don't "need" a man to survive. In the Ukraine, getting married could be an economic concession of sorts. The down side to dating Marina was that I was starting to lose the ability to speak English. A particularly common phenomena that happens to most people who visit a country where they no longer here their dialect of English being spoken. I found myself talking in a monotone Russian accent and incomplete sentences, as if I were a native Ukrainian. I was mimicking what I was hearing, which was hilarious because I was rapidly losing the ability to communicate effectively (I couldn't speak English or Russian by now) to Americans, or Ukrainians.*

*When we began our dates each evening, it was warm, and we were comfortable in short sleeve shirts, but as the Ukrainian evening faded into the night, it got cool, some nights very cool. This is useful information for all of you would-be Ukrainian Knights out there. Take a coat. As for Marina, she never got cold. But keep in mind, she is a native Ukrainian and would swim in the Black Sea in the early part of the winter. And she had no hot water in her flat, so she took cold showers in the winter. Marina was basically impervious to a little crispiness in the air. I, on the other hand, was shivering like a puppy left out in the rain.*

### Socrates of the Ukraine

*Marina was asking me many questions about America, about how I lived, about the places I visited, and the food, and on and on. As we were walking down Karl Marx Avenue on our way to dinner, she asked me what my favorite techniques (I am a science teacher) of instruction were. Good question. I told her that teachers were probably the same everywhere. Some teachers like to use the discovery method and just guide their students to the correct path. Others are harsh disciplinarians and are very regimented, like most Ukrainian teachers. I explained to her that I was neither. I consider myself to be a nurturer.*

### I'm sure my students would beg to differ, but it's my book

*I don't believe anyone learns anything from another person until you've convinced that person you genuinely care about them. I explained the word nurture again, but I could tell by the look on her face, that it was a foreign idea.*

### I think it's about to snow

*I told Marina, "If I can't tell you what it means; I will try and show you." I got very close to her face and I took both of her hands in mine and I said softly, "Marina, you are the most wonderful and beautiful Ukrainian student that I have ever had. You make me so happy just to be able to teach you. You are brilliant. I cannot wait to see you every day, because it brings me so much joy to teach you. You will change the*

*world someday, because you are so magnificent and so
wonderful. People will flock to you and stare in wide-eyed
awe at your brilliance. Future generations will speak of you
as a national heroine as you have spoken to me tonight of
your glorious heroes. Your name will be much-revered above
all others, and there will be many statues erected of you in
your homeland".*

Most of what I said was actually true. It's not like I'd
taught English to a lot of other beautiful Russian women
before now. I finally said, "Do you understand what nurture
means now?" Marina said, "It sounds like you are giving
love to others."

## Will the real terrorists please stand up?

I told Marina that she explained what nurture means
with one sentence better than I did with ten. Economy of
word usage is not my forte. I omitted the part about how
I give love to children in America, alternating with death
threats, to reinforce the notion of just how much I love them.
I'm pretty sure that some of the kids I teach in America
would be kicked out of the Islamic Jihad for being too damn
vicious. This, however, is not the end of the story. Marina
and I went on to have a wonderful dinner and we retreated
to my dwelling for, uh, more conversation. At the end of the
night, we made our way to the main square for Marina to
catch a cab. Moments before the cab arrived, she looked up
at me with those big brown eyes, took my hands and said,
"Tom, explain me one more time, please, nurture . . ."

Ok, I'm done! Put a fork in me. You had me at nurture,
Marina.

## Death becomes me

I wanted to run through the streets of Dnepropetrovsk (like one of those stupid diamond ring commercials) proclaiming to everybody, my love for the beautiful Marina. In hindsight, this would have been an excellent time to die, because I had so much adrenaline and hormone stuff coursing through my veins I'm sure any method of death that took me would have been essentially painless. At least I'm wise enough now, that "if" it happens again, I should go throw myself under a train. While it may be a premature exit from the stage, it would be the best of deaths. Because, let's face it, after you reach a certain age, you become preoccupied with the thought of having a good death. I had an old crony who liked to say that he knew the exact day he became an old person.

## Ethel, have you seen my walker, or my arthritis pills?

He got up one morning and no longer felt good enough to do what he always loved to do. NOW, you're old! Here's your sign. I am an old person. Please go stand in line over there with the rest of the old people, the grim reaper will be right with you. Never before had I experienced that much joy in one moment, excluding the birth of my children. Obviously, that's a different kind of joy.

I think it's time I give you an illustration of how Ukrainian girls treat their men.

I will tell you a story. A fateful story, no less . . .

We had been sitting at this open-air restaurant for about an hour or so, waiting on our food. It was chilly, really chilly, which made my resolve to be a tough guy that much greater.

*The more she asked me if I was cold, the more I denied the obvious, bitterly claiming I was toasty warm. Guys are such idiots. As if she couldn't see for herself I was freezing. Marina said in her Russian accented English, "Tom, tell me how is this you shiver, but you are not cold. Are you sick? Are you nervous, Tom?" Oh alright, I'm freezing. The gig was up. I felt like a girly-man, but I couldn't help it, I was cold. Marina looked at me hard, then she smiled. She got up and walked up to the owner of the restaurant, (a giant of a man who was at least as big as an NFL offensive lineman) and asked him a question. I don't think I'll ever forget the look of astonishment on that man's face. I sort of shrunk into the chair as low as I could get. He looked over at me, spoke some indeterminate Russian, (he probably asked Marina why she hung out with girly-man) and then took off his humongous overcoat that would have swallowed Andre the Giant and handed it over to Marina. She dragged the coat over to the table with both hands and then gingerly draped it over me. Half of the coat bunched up on the floor at my feet, which of course made me feel very inadequate. I can honestly tell you it was at this precise moment in time I fell in love for the second time in my life . . . Very hard!*

## Without someone to love, what is the point?

*Oh, I had been in lust a thousand times before this moment. I had kidded myself and kidded others, and cajoled women, acted shamelessly and carnally too many times to recount. I had been a great pretender and impostor, and good timing man hundreds of times before this moment. But you know as well as I do, when love strikes you, it strikes you with the ferocity of a bolt of lightning. And if you don't know the difference between a bolt of lightning striking you and all of that faking and playing around nonsense, then you obviously haven't been in love before. You are completely defenseless and completely vulnerable, and you don't care . . . There is no antidote known to man that can save you from the effects of this kind of wound. I had many emotions running around in me. Mostly, I was warm. Just kidding. When she sat down beside me again, I was overcome with emotion. At that moment in time, I would have bet my life that I was going to spend the rest of my life with this woman.*

*Love (to quote an old song) became a many splendored thing again. God, I love that word splendored, even without having the first clue what it means.*

*I know there are a lot of people out there who have not been in love even once in their life, I understand that is a fact of life for a lot of people, but I have been in love twice now. I realize there is nothing I can say to assuage that pain or that emptiness that some people have living inside of them. Any words of consolation I could produce would ring hollow in their ears. It would be a contrivance of the worst order to tell them things will be okay, like so many feel-good relationship experts and inspirational speakers do. It is preposterous social science.*

### There are worse fates to suffer than dying all alone

*Studies vary, but depending on who you believe or talk to, there will be from ten to twenty percent of the population who never get married or want to get married. But, I will say this, don't assume a defeatist attitude. It may or may not be your lot in life. Remember, keep your mind open to the possibilities. I truly appreciate my good fortune; I am not an ungrateful man. If I were to die tomorrow, I've had a beautiful life. Not that I want to die or that I don't think I could ever fall in love again, it's just that at one time in my life, my hope switch had dimmed a little. After my experiences with Marina, I am once again fully aware of the possibilities that exist.*

### I think I may have watched one too many Terminator movies

*There is no fate except for the fate you make. Don't resign yourself to a miserable, hopeless existence. Saying this is one thing, lots of people talk a good game. I'm undefeated in my mind. Aren't you?*

*Unfortunately, not only does fortune favor the brave, so does love.*

### Just a touch ripe on the vine

*My high school sweetheart didn't get married until she was thirty-nine (at an age when they say you are more likely to get hit by a meteorite then get married, I guess she stayed torn up inside for over twenty years because of me, right), but she never gave up hope. Good for her.*

## Truth or consequences?
## (Or the ball is in your court now, ladies)

*I really don't want to come across as a jerk by comparing Ukrainian women to American women. But you should know, while I am not on any sort of holy mission searching out the truth, I don't run from the truth when it finds me. You should try and remember that one. Now, I don't care who you are, that's profound. Feel free to quote me on that one. You shouldn't run from the truth, either. It just is what it is. Don't spin it, don't doctor it, and don't try to make yourselves feel better by claiming it isn't true. Because it is true. What you should be saying to yourself is, now what? Do we (as a free society) continue the slide down the slippery slope into oblivion? Or as my all time favorite word mangler Mike Tyson, once said, "I have no intentions of fading into Bolivia." I don't care who you are, that's funny.*

## Why can't we all just get along?

*Or we can do something about it. America has a fifty percent divorce rate. However, if you factor in that since 1960 when only 500,000 people lived together in this country, compared to today, when 5,000,000 people live together, (ten times as many) and at least seventy percent of these relationships will break up, but, are obviously not counted in divorce statistics, it's actually a much worse problem than it looks like on paper. America is fast becoming a country of shattered dreams and unfixable broken hearts, not only for the adults but the children caught in the crossfire. And if you can't see that for yourself, you are an idiot of unimaginable dimensions, and there is absolutely nothing I can say or anyone else can say to ever change that inescapable fact.*

### Survival of the fittest and all that rot

*American women of all people should understand the concept of competition. If you want the best men (most of the Americans I saw in the Ukraine were nice-looking men, who had money) then you are going to have to be willing to compete with Russian/Ukrainian girls to keep them. I don't care if you've spent your entire life in a university think tank analyzing the problem or you have the practical experience of getting hitched four of five times. There is a simple answer to the problem. Women have to be willing to be damsels-in-distress, and men have to step up to the plate and be heroes again. Real heroes! Come home every damn night (don't drink with your asshole buddies), support her financially and emotionally, and be there for your kids every second of every day, period.*

### Cleaning the toilet as foreplay

*And cleaning the toilet once in a while wouldn't be the end of the world for you, would it??? Got it??? So, girls, if you are willing to do your part, (which means that once in a while you will have to look in your husbands eyes with adoration instead of abject disgust) and men yours, (act like a real man should) we can fix this problem.*

## *The games children play*

But, I digress, girls. Back to my original point, that if the same situation arose in America, (boyfriend forgets coat, is freezing his ass off) an America girl would just say something like, "Well, you should freeze; you're a dumb ass for forgetting your jacket." Stop doing that! And don't say something like, "Well, he shouldn't talk to me that way, either." That's not productive, and it's the rationale a child would use to justify his bad behavior. Take ownership of your own behavior. Besides, no man is ever going to be faithful to or care about a woman who talks to him like that. So, don't blame him for running off with his adolescent secretary when he was forty. You should have been more compassionate when you had your chance. Because if you had been, that thought might have crossed his mind (to run off with his adolescent secretary), but he would have never acted on it. A man will never leave a woman who is giving him love and affection. Never!

Why?

## *Riverboat gamblers of romance*

Because, if he is guaranteed love and affection at home, he's not going to risk it all for a flip-tailed high-skirted, honey-voiced bimbette who may or may not love him. The bird in the hand principle applies here. And if your husband in fact did leave you despite your outpouring of love, then you are just in denial about your own role in the breakup.

Now your chance is gone, and all you have left is your pocket full of yesterdays to keep you warm. Well, am I right or not? You may hate me right now, but in your heart, you *know I'm right. Has there ever been an American girl in the history of America who went to the manager of a restaurant and made the manager fork over his jacket to keep her boyfriend warm???*

*Ever???*

*Even once???*

*Of course not! Don't be absurd!*

### I'm not bad; I'm just drawn that way

*I know you think I'm trying to bash American girls, and you've probably gotten your feelings hurt, but I swear I'm not, I'm merely pointing out the differences in cultures, and why an American man might be drawn in by this kind of behavior. After all, a female brain (a rose by any other name is still a rose) is essentially the same everywhere you go. But cultural differences are real and profound. There are hundreds of stories like this one. I know what you cynical types are saying out there. They just want your money, dimwit . . . Of course they're going to be sweet for a while. Maybe, maybe not. But I don't see American girls trying to be sweet to me or anyone else I know to just get their money.*

### If I was on a boat headed for a big-ass rock, I think I would change my heading

*American women are not conditioned to treat a man like this, so it's hardly their fault if they're not doting, maternalistic women anymore. I know what you're thinking, too, and you may be right. Either men have to get over their nostalgia and sentimentality or get the hell over to Russia.*

## An exodus of Biblical proportions has already began

*Well, thousands of them already have. There will be hundreds of thousands to follow. I know of a man who met two beautiful Russian girls one summer and went back to the same city the following summer to reintroduce himself to them, only to find out they had both become engaged in the interim period to other American men. You snooze, you lose, I suppose. What are the odds of something like that happening? Not as great as you would imagine.*

*Girls, I'm sure you would like a little doting paternalistic behavior out of your men, too, (touché) but you sure don't get it. True enough. Shame on your man if that's true. If that's the case you should leave his ass for the pool boy. But, I'll tell you this, good men out there are fed up and tired of paying the checks all those other jerks have been writing long before they even showed up in the store. So, we can safely conclude it would be completely understandable why a man or woman would enjoy the kind of attention I was referring to.*

## Parting is such sweet sorrow

*Marina and I came to the end of another beautiful night, and I could write many more words and many more thoughts. And I could rattle on for hours, but I know that I could never adequately describe what it felt like to be in a place like Dneproptrovsk on this summer night with*

*Marina, in that moment in time. I will only say this, and then I will leave it alone.*

*The night was complete, perfect, incorruptible, insatiable, bliss.*

## Part Two

# Fireworks on the Dnepr

*Marina and I had settled into a comfortable routine. After the coat incident had cemented our bond, I started thinking about the future, our future. Oh, Tom, you beautiful dreamer! For the road is long and there are many miles before you sleep. You haven't put Marina to bed just yet. You think it was going to be this easy to win a woman's heart?*

### Hell, my own dogs seem to always end up training me

*Just show up in the Ukraine, finance some wonderful dinners, mix in strong drink and dancing with your devastating wit and charm, and she would respond by just rolling over at your feet and playing dead like a poodle. Hah! Tom, (like most men) in the battle for hearts, you are an unarmed man. Even the straightest road will have an occasional curve.*

### It's time to finally show the hole card

*We had finally arrived at put up or shut up time. Each day had brought the promise of new ecstasies. Sleeping at night was an increasingly improbable proposition, if Marina wasn't there, not only due to the fact the sun came out at four in the morning (and I had no curtains on my windows), but I would rather lie in my bed thinking about Marina, than chance falling asleep and not thinking about her. On our next to last night together, we didn't go out. We had an intimate conversation about our future. We discussed everything. Just like young lovers do.*

### Geriatric heartthrob, maybe comrade

*It felt surreal. On the one hand, I knew I was no adolescent heartthrob anymore. I possibly had more yesterdays behind me, than tomorrows ahead of me. But on the other hand, I felt like Marina and I were acting out a part of Dr. Zhivago. A gracefully aging American man romances a beautiful and passionate young Russian girl, set against the backdrop of the Ukrainian night. Well, that's as close a reference as I could come up with.*

### A thin line separates fantasy from reality

*So the Ukrainian night stretched imperceptibly into the Ukrainian morning. Which comes real damn early as I may have mentioned before? I woke up before Marina did. I sat on the edge of the bed staring at her radiance (a friend of Marina's had told me earlier in the day that she had never seen Marina look as radiant as she did now. Which just gave me additional cause for hope) hoping against all hope that I didn't wake her up. Since I am not as eloquent as Fitzgerald, I will quote him, "A thousand phrases of pride, of passion fought on my lips seeking expression." I only knew one thing in my life for sure at this moment, that Marina loved me and I loved her, and I would have this view every morning of what was left of my life. There was but one indisputable, inescapable conclusion that could be assumed to be true, Marina was my girl. I knew that I wasn't worthy of Marina. She was perfect, myself a little less than perfect. I allowed the barely conscious thought that had begun in my mind like a mustard seed and eventually sprouted into a full-blown tree, to almost become audible. That this couldn't be real, it couldn't be possible. Only the very young, get (or deserve) fairy tale endings. Right?*

### Last dance

*Tonight will be our last night together. I will find out if Marina is indeed real, or a figment of my vaunted imagination. Had I indeed allowed my sometimes vociferous and agile imagination to run wild and free and create an illusory vision that only existed in my mind, or had I found true love?*

### Job and I were kindred spirits

*Not only had I endured the interminable year-long wait to get here, the excruciating anticipation building day by day, but now I must endure one more day.*
*I didn't pass my time idly.*

## *The best laid plans*

*For this most fateful of dinners, most fateful of nights, I chose a restaurant on the Dnepr River. One we had been to before on our first date. This day was a National Holiday in the Ukraine so I knew there would be fireworks over the bridge at dark where we would be dining. A full moon and a cloudless night were expected also. I remembered a poem I had written from my first book (the lament of the main character for a lost love from his youth, lost to the sands of time). It also contained an eloquent message of, as I so delicately put it, "the tenderness of regret." But that book and that poem was a work of fiction, this was real. Marina was real. There would be no regrets on this Ukrainian night with its full moon and blazing fireworks. I had gone as big as a man can go, almost Elvis big, (short of renting the restaurant for the night). And I had spent most of the day organizing my poem in my mind (because I didn't have my book with me, and I've written about a hundred poems) and practicing it so that I could elocute (Marina loved to say elocution for some reason) it to Marina tenderly and flawlessly as I handed her the diamond ring. All of the elements seemed to be coming together perfectly. How could any night be planned more strategically than this one? Had I left any stone unturned? Failed to dot any "I's" or cross any "T's"? My destiny would be altered tonight forever. How? Only time would tell now?*

## *It's getting throwed off that's hard to take*

*I had told myself beforehand that this would be the last time I would saddle up the horse forever. The last time I would attempt to ride off into the sunset with the girl. At the end of this night, I would either have Marina or I would not have Marina, but for sure, there would not be any tenderness of regret. I don't think you can keep falling in love over and .over. If it is truly love, then the price for loving anyone is that you must give up some part of your heart to them that you can never have back, even if you ask nicely. No exceptions. There are only so many pieces to be meted out then.*

### Underdog or overdog?

*So, let us review the plan one more time. Fireworks, check. Dinner on the river, check. Poem, check. Diamond ring, check. Rapier wit, well . . . check. Never before had a plan been so carefully thought out, planned, and executed. Success was all but guaranteed. Victory was a foregone conclusion. But, we have a belief in my native country, America. Often times on paper, one team looks invincible, and another team, inconsequential. So, they don't even play the game right? Wrong. They play the game anyway, just in case the unthinkable happens.*

*I was bringing my "A" game to the big dance, and Marina was nothing more than a pawn in my elaborate chess match, a cuddly little hare, caught in my cleverly constructed snare. I even had the foresight to have the dinner on the Dnepr River, Marina would be pinned against the banks of the river, like the Germans had the British pinned at Dunkirk. If she was going to escape my clutches, she was going to have to swim for it. Failure was not an option, like a brilliant Field General, I had deployed every weapon in my arsenal in the most strategic manner. Marina would not slip through my fingers for I left her no escape route, except the river of course.*

### It's all over but the weeping in the Borsch

*Is the suspense killing you? Well, are you at least still interested in what happened? The dinner played out exactly as I had scripted it. It was an exquisite night. No doubt, it was the greatest night of my life. I can't tell you if it was the strong Ukrainian wine, the fireworks and the moonlight on the river, or Marina's brooding beauty and thick Russian accent, but regardless of which one did the most damage, I was definitely intoxicated. I will tell you (although it pains me to) that I put on a dazzling and dizzying performance myself. My repartee was animated with equal parts charm and rapier wit. I was trying as hard as a man can, to win the heart of the fair maiden. Unlike the poem I had just read to Marina, where I tell the tragic story of the trail being littered with those who have hesitated, I did not hesitate. I had her eating out of the palm of my hand.*

### Be careful what you wish for

*The moment of truth was upon me, upon us, now . . .*

*After reciting my poem, placing the ring in front of her, and asking Marina to marry me, Marina let out a shriek of joy and turned to me with tears in her eyes. Then with tears running down her face and with a look I'm pretty sure I had never seen in a girl's face until this point in time and said, the sweetest thing. "Tom, (as she was thumbing through her dictionary) how do say in your words . . . c-o-n-v-i-n-c-e- . . .*

*Ahh, that was nice, very nice . . . Now there were two people crying, real hard.*

*Trust me, those words made all the work I had put into this evening worth it. I will always be happy I was ready to saddle up that horse one more time.*

*That I was there to hear those words and be in that moment in time was in truth, an indescribable feeling.*

*In reality, these moments are the only moments that make our existence here on earth worth anything in the first place. We suffer through so much mundane, mindless, life-numbing, spirit-sapping crap in our life just to get to this moment. You'd better savor them, people. You better store them up in your mind. They will make you smile a lot some day when you are too old for such activity, and the feelings that used to stir inside you have grown silent and still.*

### Marina has the last word

*Oh, Marina said something else. I knew I forgot something. She said an incredible thing, a very thoughtful thing. "Tom, my heart tells me you are the perfect man for me, I could listen to you talk forever. Your interlocution is wonderful, but my intuition remains silent until I see how you are with my son, Dima. Will you take his hand like you do mine, Will I finally close my eyes and rest knowing that you are protecting him like you do me? Then I will know, Tom."*

*Dang it!*

*I knew there was going to be a test involved somewhere, somehow. Up to this point it was like shooting fish in a barrel. It was too easy for me. But a kid makes it a whole new ball game.*

*Ok, let's do it. Bring on Dima.*

## Part III

# *Oh, Those Mediterranean Nights*

*On my last morning in Dnepropetrovsk I awoke at 5:00am to find that the brilliantly lit Ukrainian Sun was already burning a rather large hole in the sky. I know I'm fixated on the sun thing, but damn, it's just too early to start the day. I was temporarily paralyzed. One, from extreme fatigue, secondly from the very real fear of waking up Marina. I wanted to postpone the inevitable for as long as I could. Our goodbye scene . . .*

### To go, or not to go

*If I didn't have children of my own, I assure you I would have never come back to this country. The Ukraine and Dnepropetrovsk had everything I wanted or needed: Marina. I would have just gotten a job teaching English to Ukrainians and lived out my days trying to make Dima and Marina as happy as I could. I'm sure that I wouldn't have been the first man to forsake his homeland for greener pastures.*

### But obviously, the good kind of crazy

*Some of you surely think that I was a crazy man. Not hardly. How many millions and millions of people live their entire lives sadly lamenting the fact that they have no one like Marina to spend their days with? And it makes more sense to leave her than to find a way to stay? Of course it doesn't! Even if I stayed in Dnepropetrovsk and it all fell to pieces for Marina and myself, wouldn't I still have had a few more days of glory than I would have had otherwise? If you think about it, and I wouldn't if I were you, you would come to the same conclusion I have. Almost anyone will "tell" you they are willing to do anything for love, but when presented with the opportunity to do anything for love, they coyly, demurely decline the invitation or retreat back to what was comfortable. Very, very strange. Either you are willing to do anything for love or you are willing to do what is easy and doesn't require much effort. People love to make grandiose proclamations and outlandish protestations and incredulous pledges of undying love but sadly, it's all theatrics. It's a part of the human psyche that is unexplainable. What you should be saying is the truth. Tell your betrothed in advance the following statement. Okay baby, I will love you until someone else better-looking turns my head or has more money or you get fat, or I become restless, bored, or lose interest in you or I get sick of your mother's interference. Why not? Let your beloved have all of the factual information she deserves to have because these things are going to come out eventually anyway, and that way, if she still want to marry you after you've said what you're true feelings are, then it truly is not your fault if the marriage goes south.*

*For Lenin's sake, telling someone that you love them when you really don't is a form of stupidity I just can't wrap my mind around. Why?*

*Lying to gain someone's affection will only hurt both of you in the long run. So stop doing it!*

*If you're that lonely, get a dog! I have two.*

## **With apologies to Dr. Phil and the other relationship gurus**

*All marriages at their core are ultimately power struggles. Who is going to wrest the economic power, spiritual authority, parental authority, and generally speaking, the final word on the major decisions away from the other person. For all of this talk of equality and feminism, someone (not someones), usually has the final say in the marriage.*

*The real problem with obtaining power is that it can only be done at someone else's expense. People don't normally relinquish power freely. It has to be taken. To acquire power you must impose your will against another human. It has to be gained forcefully, purposefully, and with some malice. You may ultimately win the war, but always remember, the foe you have just vanquished was at one time your most beloved treasure, and the object of your heart's most beautiful desire. What is he or she relegated to now? The conquered combatant?*

*Most marriages end up on a descending spiral staircase. First comes the initial frustration when you are disappointed with your beloved. Possibly in the beginning of the relationship your beloved was so charismatic and physically appealing, you didn't notice that this person didn't pay attention to details (like the due date on the water and light bill) and was highly disorganized, sometimes undependable, and not always interested in doing the amount of work that is necessary to keep a marriage (every marriage) from falling to pieces.*

*Then comes the detachment, distancing, and latent hostility.*

*Then the withholding of affection rears its ugly head.*

*There's no point of return now. In the road ahead of you lies anger, frustration, blatant hostility, resentment, bitterness, and indifference.*

*You are both locked into a titanic struggle for control now. Who is going to out-maneuver or out flank the other one first? Who achieves the high ground? Who is left at the bottom of the hill with an axe to grind?*

*Now . . . there has to be a winner and a loser! It went from being a loving, committed, cooperative, blissful, relationship (early on) to an adversarial, argumentative, disconsolate morass, at light speed. Some couples never even make it past the honeymoon without an incident or a spat that exposes the façade to reveal the tiniest of chinks in the armor. Before this moment, you were both playing for the same team.*

*To give in is to admit defeat.*

*To give in is to admit weakness.*

*To give in is brilliant . . .*

*You want to be the one with the power in the relationship. But the best kind of power is benevolent, not imposing or demanding. Give it away and it will return to you. What you don't understand is that most people don't really want the power in a relationship. They are in love with the concept of power not the reality that they are so desperately trying to snatch away from your grasp. Studies indicate that almost half of the CEO's of major corporations replying to a survey, reported they were unhappy or at least discontented. Worry!!! Mucho grande worry!!! Power brings you so much control and authority you don't think about the down side. Power is responsibility, anxiety, work.*

*Hindu philosophy teaches that ambition is the root of all unhappiness. Why? Where is the saturation point of ambition, and by extension, greed? When will you ever have enough stuff to be content if you are ambitious? As the Apostle Paul would say, "an unanswerable question."*

*Most rich powerful performers are miserable. Anecdotally speaking, I've heard there is no such thing as a happy Hollywood actor. A happy actor is a mythical beast like a unicorn is a mythical beast, or an honest politician. I've also heard the same thing about the music industry. No happy performers!*

*The likelihood of angst in these professions is high; peace and contentment, low.*

*Most performers are biding their time (except for a precious few) until America loses interest in them. It's going to happen. It's just a matter of when.*

*That has to be an unpleasant feeling. That knowledge has to whittle away at their emotional stability, their self-esteem.*

*Now, for all of the regular people out there. Your spouse wants you to show a "willingness" to give up all of your power. And not just as a stupid ploy, either. If you don't mean it, your insincerity will bleed through your countenance like barbeque sauce on a white table cloth. Once they know you mean it, they'll give it right back to you.*

*This scenario is analogous to a teacher having a favorite student (every year there is some sweet little girl {or boy} that just melts your heart) and the teacher thinks they can do no wrong.*

*So, every teacher is prepared to give his power away under the right circumstances.*

*Have you ever seen a teacher be mean to his pet? He can't. He wants to grab the pet up and love him and tell him how special he is. Just like I did with Marina in Dnepropetrovisk, when I was explaining to her what nurture meant.*

*By doing this, the teacher gives the power back to the child to manipulate him, to tug at his heart, to influence his normal rational decision-making abilities. I want this child to be happy. I do not want to do anything that would damage this special bond I have with this student.*

*For you horses out there whom I have dutifully led to the water but who are still not drinking, I am talking about the interpersonal dynamics of your marriages or relationships with your significant others. The principle is exactly the same. You need to be this kind and gentle, sweet, compassionate and understanding student/ spouse who will bring power to you. People will trip over themselves to help you and to make you happy.*

*It may be counterintuitive, which is why so few people actually try this approach, (but instead opt for the bitchy, complaining, whiny-ass approach to behavioral modification, both men and women of course), but it does work. I am assuming things like, that you are in a relationship with a normal, rational, emotionally stable, non-psychotic human. Also, that you are in the same normal, rational, emotionally stable, non-psychotic condition.*

*Good people fail in their relationships all the time, not because they intend to fail or they don't care about their beloved, they fail because they don't have the first clue of how to succeed.*

*Sad! Very sad! Even tragic!*


### There will be no additional charge for this information either

*More good advice.*
*As I replayed the movie of my life, I realized something. Something big.*

*Every single time I came to a crossroads and didn't listen to my intuition, I made a mistake. What is the value of intuition if you are going to ignore it? Why do we insist on convincing ourselves that we aren't really feeling what we know we are feeling?*

*By definition, intuition is a higher form of cognitive thinking, of awareness. It just can't find its way to the conscious world. If everybody obeyed the dictates of what their intuition was telling them, the divorce rate would be cut in half in this country because fifty percent of us would have never married the person we finally married.*

*I just thought about something. If the divorce rate in this country is fifty percent, and people start listening to their intuition so that fifty percent of them don't marry the wrong person, I have almost single handedly solved the problem. That was just too simple!*

## Let sleeping princesses lie

*Back to Marina, my favorite subject. I knew two things now. That I could not stay with Marina for the time being, and that I would come back for her as soon as I could.*

*When Marina finally woke up, she must have noticed the look on my face and knew that it was the look of a man who had found paradise, but was about to give it up, she said, "Tom, why can you not stay with me? Just for a while longer. You are no longer working in the summer?"*

*Oh, sweet temptation, thy name is Marina!*

*So, Marina and I had one more tender moment, and then it was time to load my bags onto the bus and head back to the airport, back to America. It sure seemed like the ride to the airport went a lot faster than the ride from the airport when we first arrived. Marina, of course rode with me, and in the short time we had together, I tried to convey all of the thoughts and the hopes and dreams and desires that I had for the both of us. Mostly, I wanted her to believe that I was not going to just fly off into the sunset without her. I promised her that I would call her everyday from America (which due to the seven hour time differential is a major nuisance) until we were together again. I told myself that was a self-serving promise, because I had to hear her voice every day or I would have gone mad. I was willing to do anything she wanted me to do.*

### God, please don't let there be any multiple-multiple choice questions, I hate those

*I knew that I had not been able to pass the Dima test yet, but that was not a concern. Children are my passion. I never doubted my ability to win Dima's heart.*

*With all of the energy I had put into winning the fair Marina, I would gladly double my efforts with Dima. Whatever it took wouldn't be too much.*

*He would never in his life have such a good buddy as Tom.*

*The dreaded moment was upon us now. The long goodbye . . .*

*As I approached the customs agents (they didn't look so damn scary intimidating this time), my mind flashed suddenly back to a time when I was a child and I watched my dad (whom I knew would be gone for years) board a plane for Taiwan and a military stint. The sadness inside my heart was overpowering now. I didn't even want to look at Marina; I didn't want to see the hurt in her eyes. I felt like I had failed her.*

## Six of one, half a dozen of the other

*If I had loved her enough, I would have found a way to stay, even make an excuse to my children as to why their daddy couldn't come home. But, I knew how I felt all those years ago; I couldn't do this to my kids. I loved them too much. But I loved Marina, too.*

*So with an abiding anguish way down in my soul, I gave Marina one last kiss and told her that I loved her and that I promised I wouldn't forget her. That if she would just take a chance and believe in me, I would reward that faith, someday soon. She told me that she would keep my ring and when the three of us were together, she would know then if it was to be.*

## Crying in my beer, an American tradition you can be proud of

*On our flight back to America, we had a layover in Vienna. I seized the opportunity to go out with Lance and indulge in German sausage and German beer. I was always cynical about the claim of just how good German beer is. I don't even like beer, but I liked German beer. The beer was every bit as good as its proponents claimed it was. After retelling the whole tale about my adventures with Marina, Lance (who knew Marina casually) counseled and consoled me that night. He tried to encourage me about the passage of time and how wonderful it was that it happened in the first place. He finally put it to me like this, "If there is one girl in this world I would believe in, Tom, whom I absolutely know would never hurt you, it would be Marina." He was preaching to the choir. The feeling was very mutual.*

### God finally strikes back

After landing in America, I called my parents to tell them the good news that their prodigal son had returned with a fiancée and was greeted with the news that my house had flooded (hot water heater burst)while I was away, and my son (while he was unhurt) had wrecked his car. Ooh, I figured God was not happy about something.

I was good to my word. I called Marina every night. We got to know each other better and found out we had many things in common. Our life goals and philosophy of living were very similar.

I have already warned you that the story would require we take a brief excursion from the Ukraine.

Marina, of course, wanted me to meet Dima before she would talk about commitment, which was not an unreasonable request in the least. I suggested a vacation on the beautiful Mediterranean island of Malta. Due to less restrictive visa requirements for Ukrainian nationals, it was a good place to not only vacation, but also honeymoon.

### Getting all of the eggs in one basket

Well, I'm getting ahead of myself, aren't I?

I would get to spend even more time with Marina, and I would get to know Dima very well. I had an entire month to plot my strategy in my mind. To work out all of the details of what I would say or how I would respond if certain problems arose or if I was having hard time pleasing Dima. I told myself a thousand times that I had come too far, I had invested too much of myself and my emotional well-being in Marina to let a careless word or an unkind gesture, or a cultural gaffe stand in my way.

## *Elevate, Tom*

*I told myself thousands of more times, Tom; do not act like a stupid American.*

*Be a gentleman.*

*Pay attention.*

*Be on your best behavior.*

*Plant seeds of trust.*

*Listen, more than you talk.*

*Indulge her eccentricities.*

*She is a Ukrainian after all.*

*You're not in Kansas anymore Tom, or even America for that matter.*

*It's a different kind of ball game than any game you've ever played before. I remember Darrell Royal's most famous quote when he was the football coach at the University of Texas. When asked about the ferocity of an upcoming opponent, probably Arkansas (a team he had slaughtered the previous year), he said playing them at their home was like parachuting into Russia. Well, I had already done that (supposedly the hard part was over) and had absconded with two of their nationals. They would be meeting up with me in neutral territory, Malta. Neither one of us would have home turf advantage.*

*Now, what?*

### Just how good is my two step?

*I would have another country to deal with now. A completely different culture with mannerisms and customs unique to the Maltese. And a completely different set of expectations for myself. I will be playing the dual role of attentive boyfriend and doting father.*

### How many grains of sand are there on the beach?

*How many ways could I ruin this deal? Our romance might get derailed on a minor sticking point or hinge on a careless whim or idle comment. I might even get caught accidentally looking at other girls on the beach.*

*Just kidding about that one.*

### Marina was built with a sculptor's loving attention to detail, not happenstance of Mother Nature and genes

*With Marina's stupendous dimensions, looking at other girls on the beach would be like a Ferrari owner admiring a Chevy. I knew that there was the remote yet entirely possible eventuality, that at the end of the day, at the end of the vacation, at the end of my intricately laid out plans and elaborate strategy (if I won Dima's heart first, the mother's heart would be a mere technicality, a foregone conclusion, which happens to be an almost fail-proof plan), that Marina could indeed slip through my fingers like the frothy water disappearing from my grasp.*

### Roll the dice and take your chances, baby

Marina would disappear from my life forever back into the Ukraine. The odds were actually more likely that would happen, than the outcome I so desperately wanted to happen. The odds that a new relationship will end in something permanent are always the same going in. There are things that are in your control, the environment, how you act, and your choice of activities. And factors that are completely out of your control. Unforeseen incidents, travel problems, language and cultural disconnects.

### Or a really disgruntled bored scientist

Love is sort of like a mad scientist mixing chemicals from unlabeled bottles; maybe something beautiful will result from the synthesis of unknown compounds or something catastrophic and really smelly will result. Dating a lot of girls (what exactly would be the alternative?) is like people who buy multiple lottery tickets with the fond hope that it will increase their chances of winning. It doesn't matter if you buy a million tickets every week or if you date a million girls, the odds of any one of those tickets or girls being the right one is still hundreds of millions to one. The lottery people bank on our collective ignorance. As far as dating millions of girls, I call that, a nice start. So, while any effort you put into the relationship in the beginning is worthwhile and admirable, it certainly doesn't hurt your cause. If she doesn't have the right numbers, you're screwed no matter what you do.

### I'm not as good as I once was, but I'm as good once as I ever was

But I was going to bring my entire game to the table. There wasn't any reason not to. I wasn't going to leave anything in the locker room in case I had to pad up for a future attack on the fortress of a fair maiden's heart. But if it were not to be (I told myself), it would be due to factors out of my control. I would not forgive myself, otherwise. To echo the words of the late Vince Lombardi, "The credit belongs to the man who is in the arena, who strives valiantly and comes up short again and again. And if he fails, fails while daring greatly, so that his place shall never be with those cold and timid souls who know neither victory nor defeat."

I will taste victory or I will taste defeat.

It would be a short plane trip for them, a not-so-short plane trip for me, But, considering how I felt about Marina, at least, it was hardly a sacrifice.

I had to wait another month for my trial marriage/ vacation/ adventure to Malta to arrive. If I have learned nothing else in my travels, I have at least learned how to be a patient man.

At last the day of the big trip had arrived. I had been separated from Marina for thirty-three miserable days. I had called her every night (1:00 am for me) just to hear her voice. Those thirty-three days seemed ten times longer that the previous year I had waited to go to the Ukraine.

### Just add the rats

I drove to Dallas (three hundred miles), caught a plane (eight hour flight across the pond which is not for *the squeamish or stiff-jointed), landed in London, had a three hour layover, caught another plane and landed in Malta three hours later. The first thing I noticed about Malta as we flew over the island was that all of the buildings were made out of native limestone. Quite beautiful, but quite homogeneous too. As I subsequently learned, Malta resembles nothing so much as a giant maze, every street you walk down looks like the last street you walked down. I give you this somewhat innocuous information because a pivotal event in Marina's and my relationship will revolve around this somewhat nondescript fact.*

*The water is breathtaking. Iridescent blue and green.*

### My favorite form of quoting, because I don't have to look anything up

*To paraphrase Hindu doctrine (or maybe even unintentionally butcher Hindu doctrine), "you could have spent your entire life on the shore of the Mediterranean Sea, staring at its brilliant luminosity, gorgeous fusion of blue and green and pristine beauty, and you would not have wasted your life."*

*I arrived four hours ahead of Marina and Dima; I waited for them at the airport. We would only have one week together, so I had to make the most of each minute.*

*I must have looked like a statue as I stood motionless in the lobby, straining and craning my neck to see the upstairs customs and passport control area, hoping for a penultimate glimpse of both of them. I had never met Dima, so I was especially interested in seeing him.*

### Be still my fast beating heart

*My first glimpse of Marina and Dima was as they were riding the down escalator. The expression on her face was more like that of a person going in for a lobotomy than a vacation with her beloved in paradise. When we finally embraced, it was not what I had expected. Marina was overwrought. She had just traveled ten hours by train (from Dnepropetrovsk to Kiev) and five more hours by plane from Kiev to Malta with a six year old in tow. She should be overwrought.*

*That wasn't the only thing I noticed about Marina . . .*

*She wasn't wearing my ring.*

*While it may be a little premature to throw myself into the ocean, it was ominous.*

### The words logical and woman used in the same sentence. Am I good or what?

*Maybe there was a logical explanation (I told myself) for Marina to not be wearing my ring. Maybe she was afraid she might lose it in the ocean or that it could get stolen from the hotel room. Or, just maybe, it was something innocent, like she was waiting to see how Dima and I got along.*

*By the time we were delivered to our hotel room, it was quite late. We had a delicious late dinner at an ocean-front Italian food restaurant (due to Malta's proximity to Italy and Sicily, they are the dominant cultural and food influences), a brief stroll on the beach with a warm summer breeze and a Mediterranean moon smiling, and finally, regrettably we were off to bed.*

*I had managed to rationalize away the events of the day and was once again a bundle of nerves, almost giddy. After my nervous excitement from the day's events wore off, I had a peaceful slumber. I slept the sleep of the dead. It's a good thing.*

### No rest for the wicked now

*What an enormous can of worms I had unknowingly opened up by coming to Malta. I discovered early the next morning just how big that can was going to be. Marina woke me up at 6:45 am. She said, "Five minutes, Tom. We swim in ocean. Change and eat breakfast 7:30am. Walk to bus for excursion 8:15am. Return from excursion at 4:30. Change and swim until 5:30. Dinner at 6:30. Last excursion, 9:30 until midnight. Then, we get alone time." Lucky me!*

*I was actually down for all of the activities except the swimming in ocean before breakfast. But then again (as I've already mentioned), Marina would swim in the Black Sea in the winter, so she wasn't really concerned with the coolness of the water at 7:00am. If you think swimming before breakfast sounds unpleasant, trust me, it feels even worse. Once we retreated from the water, I was shivering so much that I couldn't eat any breakfast food that required me to hold a spoon of liquid. Sure, Americans love the beach, but we don't usually allow any part of our anatomy to touch the actual water until the sun has risen to a very pronounced position in the sky. At 7:00 am, the sun hasn't even said hello yet. On the upside, at least I was ready to hit the ground running after our little swim. See, I found the silver lining.*

## It is theoretically possible that I have a regimentation avoidance component in my personality makeup

*It's not that Marina upset me. I was crazy about her. I was just unaccustomed to regimentation on this scale. American men who have married Ukrainian women have a saying, "They will run your life and boss you around, and you will love them for it . . ." Hmm . . . I think if we read between the lines, I think they are saying, that Ukrainian girls will do so many other things you like (alligator wrestling) as opposed to American girls, that you can tolerate this overbearing behavior. An old bachelor friend once told me, "Sure, I'm going to get married Tom, it's just very difficult to find the perfect woman who will suck the will to live out of you slowly over forty or fifty years". Now, that's cynical. Most women can do it much faster than that. My absolute favorite quote about marriage is this, "Marriage is the triumph of imagination over intelligence". Ouch.*

## Would someone please locate a program for me?

*Additionally, we were supposed to be on a vacation. Ukrainians don't get a lot of quality vacations, so they aren't going to waste what time they do have lounging around a hotel room. Marina brought English primary reading books with her (because even on vacation, Tom, you must learn something) on the trip. Every day after our mid-afternoon swim, I would teach phonics to Dima on lounge chairs by the seaside, while Marina sunned herself. I think I loved teaching Dima as much as he loved learning English. Dima reciprocated by teaching me the Russian equivalent for each English word he learned. He cackled like a crow at my lame pronunciations. I can still hear his cackle in my mind when I want to.*

*Speaking of Marina sunning herself. On one of these afternoons I was giving Dima English lessons, and Marina was sunning herself on a lounge chair beside us. I offered Marina a foot massage. She had never had one before. Well, I'm sure you know that there are certain spots on your feet that if you rub it, you will get kind of a tingly feeling in your naughty bits. Marina really enjoyed the massage. She was moaning and carrying on like Meg Ryan eating a salad. She was beginning to irritate some of the other female tourists lying beside her, who did not come to the beach expecting a sex show.*

*After a few minutes Marina finally stopped moaning and spoke (loud enough for everyone to hear unfortunately) "Tom, why do rub that spot on my foot?" I told her that it would help her to relax and enjoy the water more. Marina said, "What do you mean relax. If you rub that spot for one more minute, I will have orgasm"*

*Silence.*

*Stone cold silence.*

*Deafening silence.*

*A noticeable hush fell over the entire Mediterranean Sea. Or at least it seemed like it did to me. Marina had the full rapt complete attention of all of the female tourists within earshot, who only seconds ago were engaged in idle chitchat. I froze in my tracks, I was speechless. I slowly turned her foot loose. Marina, hardly missing a beat, very calmly said, "Tom, why do you stop now?"*

*So I did what any compassionate boyfriend would have done. I finished rubbing her foot. And when I finished, and Marina finished, I had six bikini clad Italian girls standing in a line waiting their turn.*

*Just kidding! Well, about the bikini clad Italian girls I am.*

*The main part of that story is not that I give a nice foot massage. The point of the story (besides a little levity) is to let you glimpse into the mind of how a Ukrainian girl thinks. Orgasms are natural. Sex is natural. They aren't inhibited. They aren't repressed. If something feels good they tell you. If something feels bad, they tell you. There are no guessing games to be played with Ukrainian girls. It is refreshing and at the same time, slightly unnerving, if you are not as open or uninhibited.*

*The basic confusion about the status of this trip (extended romantic interlude or family vacation), arose from the fact that back in Dnepropetrovsk, because of her work schedule, we were only together at night and without Dima in the mix. I understood Marina's personality very well up to this point, but not her lifestyle. This trip was going to be a trial marriage of sorts. It would entail an almost twenty-four-hours-a-day relationship with a woman of a completely different cultural background and mindset, one that I had limited experiences with. Okay, it sounds like a challenge, but I think can handle it. The main thing to remember is how I felt about Marina. I assumed all of the other details would fall into place.*

*The next two or three days went off basically on schedule and without a hitch. We were seeing some amazing sights; the architecture and history of Malta are fascinating. The apostle Paul was shipwrecked here on his way to Rome for his trial. He healed the island chieftain and subsequently converted the island population to Christianity, which it has been ever since. Once again, free trivia, for your reading pleasure.*

*Marina was very good to me. In lots of ways she was good to me.*

*But I've already told you that I tell things the way they are, the way I see them, which you have either found refreshing up to this point, or you believe makes me a strong candidate for immediate institutionalization.*

## With this dagger, I strike at thine heart

*I must insert a quote from a jealous colleague at this point, to wit, "Tom, you are a real creative guy, it's just too bad your bipolar disorder interferes with your hyperactive ADD." Touché!!! With all of the unmitigated crap I dish out, it would be cowardly to not accept some of it back. Never before or since, have I been so perfectly described. There is a razor thin line that exists between charming and obnoxious, one that occasionally I will venture across.*

*I'm not going to apologize (my daddy always said apologizing is wrong if you know you're right) because the truth is what it is. I'm not purposely trying to offend any of you out there; it's just that I lost the ability to sugarcoat the truth a long time ago. What I write may not be the most palatable thing that ever crossed your palate, but trust me, it will be good for you.*

## What foul dust began to fill the air?

*The cultural differences, and thick Russian accent, which I found so endearing and charming in Dnepropetrovsk in small amounts became occasionally frustrating and exasperating. And not exasperating in an "isn't that cute how you say that word so funny way." Just plain-vanilla exasperating! Are all Ukrainian girls exasperating? Of course not! Most of them*

*(90%?) are like Elena. Incredibly charming, vivacious, old fashioned, and utterly enchanting.*

## Tom will now attempt to balance milk bottles on his feet while standing on his head

*You just have to keep in the back of your mind, that while this was technically a "vacation," I was on a Mediterranean Island with predominantly Italian people having to deal (in business transactions and restaurants) with their unique mannerisms (volatile and aggressive at times), a girlfriend from another country (with mild language barriers to deal with), a very active six-year-old non-English-speaking boy, and a complicated public transportation system. I had to keep everyone entertained and fed and make sure that there were no glitches in the program.*

*So . . . Maybe some exasperation was already built into the trip*

## These tasks would be a lot easier to accomplish if I were twenty

*Truthfully, Marina only became exasperating to me when I started having a hard time getting things done.*

*She certainly wasn't exasperating back in Dnepropetrovsk. She was exquisite. We were exquisite together.*

## With all of these rocks, there's got to be sand somewhere

*As I mentioned, the public transportation system was a little complicated for a stupid American. Many different buses and bus stops had to be coordinated in order to get to a particular destination. Maybe a sandy beach (because most of Malta is rocky), a tour of a fifteenth century cathedral, the fish market, a carriage ride, boating, ferry ride to another island, etc,*

*Marina would not be happy with me if I had not calculated everything precisely. She would show her unhappiness by expressing a sort of indifference to what I was saying. Ukrainians do like efficiency. She would not be content to just meander on the shore soaking up rays and just enjoying my company. She wanted lots of action.*

*Now for the major malfunction associated with the streets. On one of our afternoon walks through the streets of Malta, we stumbled upon a Turkish Restaurant that Marina wanted to have dinner at later. Well, we continued on for hours meandering though the narrow streets sight-seeing and window-shopping. No harm done yet.*

## Paying attention to details, priceless

*Later that afternoon after our swim, we got dressed for dinner and went out on the town. I couldn't find the exact restaurant we had stumbled upon earlier in the day. We always thought it was going to be around the next street corner. I hadn't bothered to get the name of the street it was on earlier in the day. Marina was not happy. Big mistake. Unlike most guys, I asked for directions to avoid future agitation. Some of the directions were wrong and took us nowhere and some of the directions were to other Turkish restaurants. At some point in the festivities Marina's indulgences of my ineptitude was finally exhausted. "Tom take me anywhere and feed me, I do not care."*

*Okay, this is something I can do.*

### The plot thickens

*I proceeded to the nearest restaurant and asked to be seated. Marina looked at the menu and concluded that they did not have the right kind of soup for Dima. She was disgusted by now and informed me that she was now too tired to eat and headed off to bed with Dima. I had failed her and Dima. Despite my best intentions, I had started the evening behind and could never catch up. Once I didn't locate the restaurant in an appropriate time window, it was over. There would be no alone time tonight for Tom.*

### Fate can be a fickle friend

*In a miraculous twist of fate, she emerged from her slumber about an hour later and declared she was ready to eat again. Mortified at the possibility of disappointing her again, in the interim period I had secured actual directions to the restaurant at the source of the conflict to begin with.*

*Sweet redemption.*

## *Sweetness personified*

It turned out to be about the best food I had ever eaten in my life and Marina and Dima liked it as well. Sweet little Dima told Marina to tell the owner something for him. He told his mother to tell the owner that when he grew up, he would come back to Malta, and he would bring his family and they would eat all of their meals in this one restaurant. The kid was impressed with the food. He made the owner cry.

That was a nice moment.

I am not sure how this next incident ties into my story, other than I want to show you just what a clever boy Dima is, and also that it is a fascinating expose on how Western culture (specifically America) affects other peoples of the world. It will also serve as an additional explanation of why I did what I did in relation to Dima at the end of our trip to Malta.

## *God better have a blindfold on*

The three of us were in a very ornate very beautiful fifteenth century cathedral. There were mosaics depicting Bible passages adorning the floor, extending all the way to the ceiling.

Women even had to remove their shoes if they had spiked heels. Now Marina was not a Christian, but she was moved by the beauty of her surroundings. Keep in mind this conversation transpired in Russian, Marina translated later for me. She began and elaborate ritual of covering all of her exposed body parts in scarves, and she leaned over to Dima, who was sitting beside me on a bench and said the following, "Dima, I will go into the sanctuary and ask God for you one *thing, only one thing, I will not ever do it again. You must think about the one thing you want in life and I will ask God for it. You should not always ask for things. Just one thing, Dima. What do you want?"*

## The concept of God as a really nice department store

*You should have seen the look on Dima's face; he must have been thinking God was going to hand over the goods right then and there. Now Dima's response I understood because he replied to his mother in perfect English with the following words:*

*IBM computer.*

*Isn't that a scream? Marina almost fell down she was laughing so hard. Me, too, but only after Marina explained to me what had just transpired.*

## Gestapo strategies for new mothers

*The best way I can describe Marina's mothering skills is to say she was indulgent about certain things and indifferent about others, often in the same breath. Marina was kind of cross between a real hardass drill sergeant and Mary Poppins. The only pattern I could find was that if Dima complained about something (like he was tired of walking) Marina would make him continue to walk or if his feet got hot on the pavement after swimming and he complained, she would make him stand even longer on the sidewalk burning his feet or if he said he was hungry, she would be reluctant to feed him right away. She seemed to punish Dima harshly (as if to send a message, I will not reward your whining) for acting out or complaining, but lavished him with praise when he would study his English lessons with me, for instance.*

## Mutt and Jeff

*Dima and I were inseparable. He ran my legs off at the beach and swimming out in the deep water. He was Ahab to my Moby Dick as he rode my back out in the deep water as we looked for imaginary (thank God) sharks to devour. I can still remember some of the Italian tourists commenting on what a good father I was when they noticed how much I was running up and down the beach with Dima. Right!!! That's me. Father of the Year!!!*

*Of course I had some ulterior motives in being his playmate. Marina and I only got alone time when Dima went to sleep. It was in my best interest to run him to death during the day. Occasionally, I would have to poke him in the ribs (when Marina wasn't looking) to keep him from falling asleep on the buses. I whispered in his ear, "Dima, you aren't tired. No naps for you, Dima! You need to sleep later, when it can do both of us some good." I just wanted to make sure Dima got his money's worth on this vacation. That's all I care about; really it is.*

*I was only kidding about the ulterior motive angle.*
*Ahem!*

*I'll tell you one thing-this kid was a pistol. He was something else. He had a major fixation on food, too. Probably because he was so poor (almost all Ukrainians are poor by American standards), he had very little variety of food in his diet back in the Ukraine. The Ukraine is the only one of the Russian satellite countries with a growing season.*

*But they still only have certain foods during the season it is grown.*

*It was during our quiet times at dinner and lounging by the seaside, that I learned the most about what Marina was like as a mother. Some of her mothering skills were impressive. Dima was never allowed to drink soda, which is an excellent health practice to maintain. I know that we walked several miles one morning to locate fresh fruit and juice drinks for Dima. Marina also made me eat fresh fruit. Refusing wasn't exactly an option. Ukrainian girls are like American girls in the respect that they have the same ability to make you feel foolish if you don't do what they ask you to do.*

### Battan Death March Part II

*One time, after a particularly grueling walk up and down Malta's side streets, Dima put up his outstretched arms toward me indicating he wanted to be carried for awhile. His eyes looked so sleepy. He had held out as long as he could. I would have carried Dima barefoot across a coral reef if he asked me to. At about the same time I reached down to scoop him up, Marina grabbed me roughly by the arm and said to me, "Tom, I will tell you one time only, Dima is a strong boy, he is no baby. He can walk like we do, do you understand me?" I believe she elocuted her sentiments quite succinctly, don't you?*

*I really do understand the principle behind tough love and not giving in to kids. My God, in America, you will see kids screaming their heads off in department stores and restaurants until they get their way.*

*I guarantee you one thing; Russian kids do not pitch hissy fits. Or if they do, they get a ton of bricks dropped on their frickin' heads.*

*Dima was a six-year-old boy on forced marches, of course he got tired, I was even exhausted. My heart would break for him sometimes. I was with him such a short time I wanted to cover him with love. I guess I had no interest or inclination in being a hard-ass temporary dad.*

## Let them eat cake, or at least let the Russian kid with Tom have some

*Another amusing story associated with food and Dima took place when we were on another one of our walking safaris. By the way I don't know how long you would have to walk to get a Ukrainian girl tired (see Elena and Tom in Dnepropetrovsk for additional reading reference) because no one has ever successfully completed that mission. Anyway, Dima was walking between Marina and myself and looked up at his mother and said (in Russian of course), "I know you didn't ask me but I have a little money in my pocket to put with yours, if you want to buy me a piece of cake." Just try resisting a little cad like that. What a sweet boy. Dima was wiggling his way into my heart faster than a speeding Ukrainian cab hits an off ramp. I told Dima that I wanted to buy him three pieces of cake. I did and then he ate them.*

## The kind of place, that if you don't have a jacket, they give you one

The last incident involving food occurred at Gillerus'. Gillerus' is strictly a coat-and-tie kind of place. Surely, it had to be the classiest restaurant in Malta. The waiters look like they could have been Donald Trump's butlers. Very elegant. Not the kind of place you could or should order a hamburger. Ordering a hamburger at Gillerus', would be like asking to see the paint by numbers wing at the Louvre.

The ambience is well . . . Mediterranean. It's also located in a small alcove with literally hundreds of sail boats anchored in the bay.

## You really should have been there

Very picturesque. What? Picturesque on a Mediterranean island, surely I jest?

## You can remember so much more with mental notes and a camera, rather than just mental notes

I consciously told myself to take as many mental notes of what this place looks like and try to remember how I feel as much as I could, without ignoring Dima or Marina. I knew that at some point in either the near or distant future I would want to remember all of the details of what happened on these nights. It's hard to say if those Mediterranean nights were as beautiful in reality as they were in my mind. I was in a heightened state of emotion and physicality, and every other way a person can be heightened.

*There is never a day that goes by in my life when I don't think about what happened in Malta. It may be something small, like when I eat a piece of cake I think about Dima eating those three pieces of cake, or when I see an image of the ocean, I think about what the Mediterranean looked like or when I eat fish, I think about the world famous fish market in Valetta or if I see a boat, I think about the ferry ride to Gozo or a fireworks stand, I think about the (details to follow) Festival of Lights.*

*Sometimes it's something big, like the times I catch myself daydreaming (when I'm supposed to be teaching, dammit) about Marina and how she looked and how she made me feel when we were alone.*

## If you've ever read "Watership Down," you are not going to like this part

*The reason why we dined there in the first place was that I had found out Gillerus' was one of the few restaurants on the island that served rabbit. Rabbit is the national dish of Malta. If it is indeed the national dish of Malta, why do only a few restaurants serve it? Good question.*

*Marina wanted to try it. She liked it so much that we ate there three nights in a row. They also serve a really nice white bread for appetizer too. Probably sourdough bread. On our last night at Gillerus', our last night in Malta, they were slow getting the bread to the table. Dima asked his mother "What would we have to do to get some bread around here?" Enchanting, I tell you. Remember, Dima was six. There was definite major male bonding going on between Dima and myself even though he spoke no English. Marina, however, was like reading an exquisitely long novel. It's definitely worth the effort, but there are probably going to be some lulls to endure before you get to the finish line.*

*It was on these nights, after we had dined at Gillerus' that Marina would grow soft toward me. I've learned very little about women over the years, except that there is usually one thing that you can do for them or that you can say, that will illicit a special response. The trick of course is to discover what that one thing is before your girlfriend discovers you are so inept that you will never figure it out, and she dumps you.*

## If it weren't for all the dang trees, I could see the forest

*Girls are very conscious of what you choose to remember about them. If you can't even remember the big stuff, the things that make them happy and feel good, then you are just a soon to be fading memory in their hearts, waiting for your ticket to get punched. Guys in general are notorious for not paying attention to any of the important details in relationships.*

*Big, big mistake. Women will never understand that just because you can't remember every detail of their life history, that it doesn't necessarily follow that you don't care about them. It has more to do with genetics and the wiring of a male brain versus a female brain than about any issue of love or concern.*

*Scientists have just recently documented over one hundred structural differences between male and female brains.*

*My point being, that Marina's hot spot was getting to eat at Gillerus'. It's doubtful she had ever been treated to that level of elegance in her life.*

*So after dinner each night, we would walk back along the shore to the hotel under a glimmering moon.*

*Marina would put Dima to bed and come visit me. After our visit, Marina and I would sneak up to the upstairs dining room and go out on the hotel balcony that faced the Mediterranean. I would just wrap my arms around her and look out at the sea; sometimes compare its brooding dark magnificence to Marina's brooding dark magnificence. Of all the things I got to do in Malta with Marina, and with Dima, this is the one image that will haunt me. I do go down by the shore later as you will discover when Marina has to go to be with Dima. But these nights on the balcony were the defining moments. How wonderful would it have been to never leave this place? To always be on this balcony holding Marina.*

*I compared the whole experience with Marina to being at boot camp during the day but being able to go off station at night.*

### Some enchanted Mediterranean evening

*Some of our evenings were on the spectacular or surreal side. The Festival of Lights (honors the Apostle Paul's conversion of the island inhabitants to Christianity)) celebration stands out. After a particularly wonderful day filled with swimming in the ocean, eating and sightseeing, we took a bus ride into the capital of Valetta. The fireworks and music went on into the wee hours of the morning. It was an exquisite festival replete with marching bands, people dressed in period costumes, native delicacies served by sidewalk vendors, tours of the ornate cathedrals, and one ceremony after another. The night almost literally never ended. Dima rode on top of my shoulders (I guess the warden was feeling charitable because we were at a festival) most of the night. I have never seen a little boy so excited and so happy. He finally gave up the ghost around 3:00am, and fell asleep in my arms while Marina and I were sitting on the balcony of a restaurant taking in the extravaganza.*

*Never before have I been part of such a magical night.*

### Well, it couldn't all be good

*Remember what I said about eating the fried chicken? There will always be the element of taking the good and bad inherent in these kinds of relationships. As I've already mentioned, romantic bliss aside, the cultural differences are always going to be part and parcel of dating foreign women. Marina just happened to be a Ukrainian woman, with the particular cultural influences all Ukrainian women carry around.*

### Night falls in the Mediterranean

*The long goodbye.*
*How many books have been written about it?*
*How many love sonnets have been penned throughout history to immortalize it?*
*How many poets have coughed up their guts, and bled out through their hearts lamenting their unrequited loves?*
*I have no idea, but it's got to be a lot.*

*The second big moment in our relationship was fast approaching. Our last goodbye . . .*

## *You go your way, I'll go mine*

*I think we both knew at this point that we were not going to get married. I believe that a good general rule of thumb to follow is that if your fiancée is so demanding and frustrating and hard to please that you get stomachaches, (which up to this point in time I never got), then, maybe, it's not meant to be.*

*I remember a line from a book, (I just don't remember the book) that stated the postulation a person should seek out a mate that calms the turbulence in their soul and doesn't challenge it to a fight. In the continuum between calming my soul and challenging it to a fight, Marina was on the wrong end of the continuum. I mentioned earlier in the book that the first forty years of my life were spent in warfare; spiritual, domestic, and personal. If I had married Marina, this warfare would have mostly gone on unabated the rest of my life with momentary respites of romantic ecstasy. Which happens to be a tradeoff I'm no longer willing to make. I really, really need, (or at least want) peace, contentment, and emotional stability with a future mate significantly more than I want a raging woman. The Bible very clearly states in Proverbs, that it is better to live on a rooftop in the desert, than live with a raging woman. Leave it to God to put things in the right perspective.*

## *One man's pampered princess, is another man's hellcat*

*That sounds so much harsher than I mean it. What I'm trying to say is that with such vastly different levels of expectations for one another and vastly different life experiences, that's how Marina made me feel. Maybe, it was mostly self-imposed. Maybe another man would have embraced her idiosyncratic behavior and eccentricities. I remain completely open to the notion that the failure of the romance was as much my fault as hers. If you asked Marina, she might say the same thing about me. I mean, after all, a guy with a bipolar disorder and hyperactive ADD can probably tax even the most patient Ukrainian girl. I'm not trying to assess blame or fault. I'm attempting to explain why something that had started out as such a great romance in the hills of Dnepropetrovsk, could easily wash up on the beaches of Malta.*

*I was scheduled to catch an 8:00am flight out of Malta the next morning. Marina and Dima still had one more day left because of their flight schedule. In order to get to the airport and check my luggage on time (international flights require you be at the airport two hours before takeoff), I had to leave the hotel by 5:00am.*

## *I think the technical word for it is closure*

*I wanted Marina to let me stay with her on this last night together. Just to lie beside her and hold her one last time. Dima was going to be in a bed beside us, so I wasn't asking for any special favor. Marina knew it was unlikely we would ever be together again. Even if I lived in Dnepropetrovsk, we* knew that our romance had run its course. She may have still had strong feelings for me, but they weren't enough to overlook my faults and inadequacies, or at least that's what I supposed to be true. I didn't think what I was asking Marina to do, was out of line.

Marina however did. She just said no.

## A woman's perogative

In your life there will occasionally be moments that strike you with the ferocity of a fist in your stomach. This was one of those moments. I stood there stunned for a few seconds.

I was hoping she was kidding.

I should have known better.

I asked her why I couldn't stay, and it didn't help soothe my bruised tender ego that she really didn't have a reason. She made something up on the spur of the moment, like she couldn't sleep if I were there.

Which wasn't true.

She had slept beside me plenty of times before this night. But as far as I was concerned, why she didn't want me to stay was a moot point. The fact that she didn't want me to stay at all is what ground up my heart and crushed it into little pieces. Slight over dramatization.

She asked me to come wake her up and tell her bye the next morning, which I thought was kind of a mixed signal of sorts.

## *The politest way of saying I don't love you*

*With a kiss goodnight, she left my room.*

*I went back to my room and barely slept. I was wounded emotionally, maybe even traumatized. It's hard to say for sure, because when your emotions get involved in a moment like this one, you tend to lose your perspective, or get slightly detached from the reality of the moment. Sort of like people who are involved in traumatic events like car wrecks; they say everything moved in slow motion.*

*I had come to Malta with the expectation of marrying Marina and honeymooning while we were here. I ended my vacation by flying back to America still single and alone. And it doesn't matter to me if I read one million pop psychology rags that advocate the joy of solitude and being alone, and just loving yourself. They are all full of shit. Believe it. There is no joy in loneliness, in solitude. A life not shared, is a life only half lived.*

*Being alone is just that, lonely, someone a lot more famous than me once said, "The person who tries to live alone will not succeed as a human being. His heart withers if it doesn't answer another heart. His mind shrinks away if it hears only the echoes of his own thoughts and finds no other inspiration".*

*Take that, you relationship gurus!*

*I got up early the next morning and debated whether I should wake her up or not. To be honest, I had my feelings hurt so badly, I didn't want to tell her bye. I rationalized that if I didn't mean any more to her than that, then I would rather not tell her bye.*

### *It provides a lovely view doesn't it?*

*I could have taken the high ground.*

*I could have swallowed my pride and went up there, gave her a big hug, and told her the truth.*

*I'm sorry it didn't work out, that I will always love you (which doesn't mean you can't ever love again, you just have to let that person have the part of you that you freely gave to them that I told you that you can't get back) and I will cherish what time we did have together.*

*That's the high ground.*

*You know I'm a big proponent of taking the high ground in relationships. It does you no good on any level to try and match someone else's supposed bad behavior with bad behavior.*

*Tit for tat is always a doomed strategy.*

*Psychology 101.*

*Showing anger or hostility or disdain toward someone who has offended you; or withdrawing your affection, or detaching yourself from the relationship will never, never, never resolve the conflict. Finding out why they are behaving the way they are, is the only thing that will resolve the conflict. Period. External conflicts can almost always be resolved by fixing what is wrong internally with the combatants.*

### *I know what you're thinking. If you're a guy and somebody mentions invisibility. It's autonomic. Girls' locker rooms*

*Or as the psychologists like to say, "The problems that you have in the visible world where you live are manifested by what is going on in the invisible world where your emotions live, your head and heart."*

*I could have just assumed that it just wasn't to be. I could have elected to hold no grudge for Marina's real or imagined slight from the previous night.*

*I'm not proud of how I felt, but in my mind, I had tried my best to make Marina happy, and I just couldn't do it.*

*Maybe not saying bye to her was even out of spite, maybe it wasn't, and maybe it just doesn't matter why.*

*I couldn't sense any opportunity to resolve our differences.*

*I couldn't find the right door to enter.*

*I knew in my heart, I never would.*

*I was at a loss for words, for ideas, for deeds.*

*I didn't tell her bye either.*

*My heart wasn't in it.*

*Not at that time.*

*Not in that moment.*

### An international incident just waiting to happen

*Not after everything that had transpired between us.*

*Especially after I had moved Heaven and Earth to be with her and Dima in the first place. But in my defense I did go to her room and slide a note under the door for Dima. At the very least, Dima deserved something from me; he gave me so much love, that I thought about snatching him away from Marina and bringing him to America to raise. I had written the note in Russian with the help of a Russian dictionary. I promised Dima that I would send him some things from America, and I expressed to him how I had grown to love him so much in such a short time and that nothing would have made me happier than if I could have been his father. I told him that in the future, when he was a grown man, I would pay for that trip back to Malta that he wanted to take with his own family, and that we would eat every dinner at the Turkish restaurant he loved so much. I meant it, too. I didn't say those things to hurt Marina, I really want to see Dima again, and I will.*

*Hindsight tells me I should have taken the high ground.*

*I think I finally, once and for all, have convinced myself that alligator wrestling can only take you so far in a relationship; incompatibility will eventually do even the most torrid love affair in. My theory, I guess it's mine, is this: when you are twentyish, you desperately want marriage and kids because you have a social, cultural, biologically-programmed response to want it. I know I did. As long as I was in love, the issues or differences we might have had were immaterial. She was so beautiful I didn't care if we were compatible.*

### Of course, there are probably worse mistakes a guy can make (like say Olga the quarterback)

*Well, incompatibility isn't a river in Egypt?*

*So I made the same mistake again. I sought out a ravishingly beautiful woman, and we had zero compatibility. Well except the part about how wonderful she thought I was. I think we were very compatible on that issue. Sadly, while it is true you will never experience the passion with an American girl you would experience with a Ukrainian or Russian girl, it's essentially the same difference between riding a thoroughbred and a pony. A pony may try hard, it's just has no chance of ever being a thoroughbred. You will however, have an easier time understanding an American girl.*

### Why fix something that's not broken?

*Having said that, she's still going to be an American girl: extremely assertive, sometimes demanding, aggressive, hostile, materialistic, indifferent, and hard to please. Although I will entertain the notion that pleasing a woman of any nationality will always prove to be problematical. As my favorite guru Lance is fond of saying, "Stereotypes are stereotypes for a reason, but in every culture there is still a wide range of randomness of personality traits." In defense of American girls, you will have a preexisting commonality of beliefs with them. As far as being able to find sweet American girls, certainly, I raised one myself. They're not all bad. Is there in fact an inverse correlation between the level of sweetness you can expect from your wife and the number of years you've been married, or not? Hard, statistical, verifiable, provable evidence is hard to come by; anecdotal evidence passed between men could probably fill every book in every library in the world. With American girls you will have a recognizable foundation to build on. Your common cultural reference points will lend themselves to more effective communication.*

### Or at least, that's what some woman told me

*The backbone of any healthy relationship is communication.*

### Female translation: Childish

*My personality type tends more toward playful, irreverent, informal, easy-going, and loosely structured. Unfortunately, due to the fact that Ukrainian girls have to put up with Ukrainian men who are extremely undependable and unreliable, they would prefer their men to be on the serious side. A sense of humor is fine, but you'd better mean what you say and say what you mean.*

### A firing squad would have been much quicker and less painless

*There were many days I felt nervousness in my stomach because I was afraid of saying the wrong thing or I was worried that I was not living up to Marina's expectations. It was an abnormal pressure I put on myself. This pressure kept me off balance. It was sometimes difficult to relax completely around Marina.*

### Off I go into the wild blue yonder

*As I loaded my luggage into the back of the cab and we slowly drove off, I looked out at the Mediterranean (hoping that some of my pain would wash out to sea) one last time, and then back at the hotel where Marina and Dima were sleeping. I was thinking about what I had lost and what might have been, and where do I go now?*

## I hate Shakespeare

*So, it's better to have loved and lost than to have never loved at all . . .*

*I have loved and lost twice in my life now.*

*The loving part is wonderful, but the losing part is sure getting hard to take.*

*In these affairs of the heart, the philosophical angle is the only one that will save your mental health and emotional stability.*

## Wherever you are tonight, thank you, Gary Busey

*I'll never know for sure why things didn't work out between Marina and me.*

*Some things in life just are.*

*Maybe Marina was never serious about me to begin with. Maybe it was an elaborate ruse (the grand romance in Dneprpetrovsk that is)on her part to get a vacation out of me. Maybe she was faking with me to get what she could. Although, if that's true, Marina was an incredible actress. And Ukrainians are known more for their brutal honesty than deception. Maybe I wanted to believe that so that I could absolve myself of any of the blame or the guilt of not doing all of the little things she expected of me.*

## Well, it didn't sound corny at the time

*I left a big part of me when I flew out of Malta that morning. As I stood on the steps of Malta's international airport waiting for my plane, I finally remembered* something I had told Marina in Dnepropetrovsk. When I gave her the ring I said "This ring has my heart inside it. Do with it what you please. Either wear it and keep my heart with you always or throw it away. I don't want my ring back. I don't want my heart back."

### Really, you can trust me this one time

So, with that in mind, this next statement is going to sound contrived. Just like the sort of a thing a writer would come up with for a dramatic exclamation point to his tale. Oh, how I wish it were fantasy. If only I didn't have to live through the actual moment. It was pain I'm not going to even try and describe with mere words. A famous author once said, "The deepest emotions, the one that sustain you and nurture you, can only be felt and never spoken." Actually, I wrote that, but back to the story. I had my walkman with me, and in attempt to get Marina off of my mind and what I had just remembered about my heart and the ring, I turned it on.

### Now, I hate Kenny Chesney to

A very beautiful Kenny Chesney song was the first one to play. It went something like this. "I knew I could never hold the girl, she was built to see the world, trade winds blowing through her hair, bag of sea shells in her hand, sunlight dancing in the water, I wish I was there, she's on the coast of somewhere beautiful, running with my heart."

Ouch, ouch, ouch, ouch, ouch!!!

### Every rose has its flesh-piercing thorns

*If that isn't the most ironic, coincidentally timed song in the history of romance that I have ever heard, then my ass is a typewriter. With apologies to Lewis Grizzard. I don't want to say God was rubbing my nose in it, but it sure seemed that way at the time. I was stupefied and completely lifeless. Oh, I boarded the plane eventually with my physical body and made my way back to the United States, but I had left something behind in Malta. Something I will have a hard time doing without. Marina.*

*Marina, and Dima.*

*While it is obviously true that you may never have to experience this level of pain if you never expose yourself to the vagaries and uncertainties associated with giving your heart so completely over to another person's whims.*

### You know, I need to talk to someone about my horse fetish

*You will never really know for sure if you are alive or not, either. Believe me; I've known a lot of middle-aged people who died long before their time. Except it was their spirit that was laid low, not their actual body. They refused to saddle up that old dusty roan one more time for one more gallop around the pasture. To bad. I guess standing on the sideline watching the rest of the world play ball is a choice that some people are quite content with. Not me, not ever.*

*I quote a fellow expatriate, Lance, one more time, for posterity, "Just because something has never happened, doesn't mean it isn't going to happen." Amen! One of my favorite lines in an old country song says it so much more eloquently than I ever could, "I'm going to fall in love again tonight, for the last time . . ."*

## The never ending story

*I left off one aspect of the trip.*

*After Marina and I had hung out on the balcony awhile, and she left me to go be with Dima, I would slip down to the hotel bar later for a nightcap. I had developed a friendship with the old guy who ran it. He would give me a cold something and I would retell the biggest moments of the day. I could tell they were wistful moments for him. He was well past the age of romancing Russian beauties. But he sure liked hearing about it from someone who wasn't. He could hardly suppress the grin on his face while I was talking. Some nights I had to pinch myself. I was vacationing on a Mediterranean island with a goddess. You'd be wistful, too. Yes, at times the cultural differences and my ineptitude put a damper on things, but all in all, we had some big moments.*

*After visiting with the old guy, I would continue my late night prowl by going down by the shore.*

## Any ideas, God???

*I sat on a massive rock watching the black wave's incessant pounding of the shoreline. I peered out into the vastness of the sea as the moon overhead (complicit with me) held its vigil as my silent companion. The only discernible sounds were those of a distant dance club (with young nubile types partying deep into the night) and the crash of the waves.*

*Being by the sea is such a complete feeling. The dark sea, which seems so infinite during the day, is so much more infinite at night. Its mysterious and perilous blackness is at once foreboding, and yet comforting from a close yet safe enough proximity. The sea represents so much life and death.*

*Possibly, the greatest conundrum of all.*

*The sea is the giver of so much life, so imposing, so majestical, yet unforgiving, cruel, and full of death, all at the same time.*

*Shelley once wrote, "The earth and ocean seem to sleep in one another's arms, and dream."*

*Nice.*

*I once wrote that regret is a road that has no end. It's the only emotion you will never find any relief or peace of mind from feeling. It is what it is. The conscious part of your brain tells you that you did something wrong or that you had a moment in time that you could have seized, but instead you let it go. How many moments had I let go with Marina, how many things that I said and did would I change now? Regret is the worst form of mental torture.*

### I've got just the right memory bank all picked out

*Obviously, I did some things right along the way, too.*

*I will have to be a very old man with advanced Alzheimers disease before I forget what those nights felt like. First, the elegant dinner at Gilleru's, the stolen rendezvous with Marina in my room and on the balcony, schmoozing the old guy, and finally spending what was left of the night, by myself, down by the shore. Yes, I was alone at the shore, but I was full of hope. I could sense the possibilities; they were that tangible. Hope dies a slow lingering death. Another profound statement for those of you keeping count. I was like Gatsby, who had come so far, and so close to his dream, how could he fail to grasp it now?*

### Curse you, Gatsby

*But like Gatsby, my dream was behind me. Except mine, was left somewhere in the vastness of the Ukraine and Dnepropetrovsk . . . and Malta. I searched my heart for anything that would help me to retrieve my dream. To undo that which was already done. To rewrite the tale and switch out the happy ending where the girl and the boy ride off into the sunset, for the one where the boy is left on the shore grasping at hope and yesterday.*

*I hope that I will at least always be able to go back to Malta in my mind (if Dima says nyet) and that I will always be able to conjure up the illusory image of Marina in my arms, the ocean spray crashing into the rocks, and the moon illuminating the dark sky and the even darker water, throwing down just enough light to somehow soften the darkness creeping in on my soul.*

### I wish I'd said that

*Even more to the metaphorical point, a favorite quote from F. Scott, "The sun went down with a riotous swirl of gold and varying blues and scarlets, and left the dry rustling night of Western summer. Dexter watched the even overlap of the waters in the little wind, silver molasses under the harvest-moon. Then the moon held a finger to her lips and the lake became a clear pond, pale and quiet. There was a fish jumping and a star shining, and the lights around the lake were gleaming".*

*Spendid!*

*So, in that one respect you may be ahead of people like me who are always willing to chase a dream, to invest their entire health and emotional stability and well-being in another person, and to hang it all out on the line for the entire world to see your folly. You know it sure doesn't sound like such a good idea when I put it that way, does it?*

## Marina has left the building

*So, our great love affair that had bloomed like the most perfect flower on the banks of the Dnepr River back in Dnepropetrovsk, had all too soon faded and died in the heat of the Mediterranean sun. In time, maybe I won't be sad it ended. I'll be happy because I got to spend part of my life with a goddess, a person who made me feel the way I was certain I would never feel again.*

# Chapter Nine

## Lance rides off into the Ukrainian Sunset

*I said at the beginning of this book that I was an expatriate in training.*

*Most of this book was written about the events from the previous summer. Obviously it took me several months (about eight) to organize my thoughts and sort through my feelings and assemble this book into a cogent accounting of everything that had transpired between Marina and myself.*

*A new summer is upon me now.*

*A new chance at redemption, perhaps.*

*My theory (as if anyone else would want to claim it) is that most of us spend our youth and young adulthood bumbling, fumbling, and stumbling blindly through the dark (with little direction, and little purpose, we are at the top of the consumption food chain, bottom of the production end) wiling away the hours in bohemian hedonistic lives and the pursuit of unhealthy and less than wholesome activities and then subsequently, are forced to spend what is left of our lives looking for redemption.*

*Fitzgerald will serve as our final authority on this subject. I personally feel that almost all of Fitzgerald's works involve this particular phenomena, this foible of the human condition, if you will.*

*I told you earlier in the book that I am on no mission seeking out the truth (because you are more likely to find an approximation of it if you don't try too hard), but in those rare times when it found me, I didn't run away either. Buddha put it this way, "If you will now at all times, whether walking, standing, or lying, only concentrate on eliminating analytic thinking, at long last you will inevitably discover the truth."*

*I feel like my training is complete now. I have pondered my future in America and weighed it against my future in the Ukraine. I've examined the cold hard facts (through the clearest prism I could find) of what day to day living in another country really means.*

*It isn't all good.*

### My Kingdom for a chicken fried steak

*The food certainly will take some getting used to because you can't be eating at Tavern on the Dnepr every night. Not when you are working for Grivnas, instead of dollars. The language barrier is just that. Although not an unhurdleable barrier, there are times when you really wish you knew more Russian or they knew more English. And I never really wanted to live in a climate like Minnesota. Which begs the question, why do Minnesotans?*

*But on the good side, I will get to see Dima again. That fact alone almost makes it worth chucking it all in and heading across the pond.*

*If all of you out there could be completely honest with yourself, you would admit there are many things about*

*America you don't like. I'm sure some of you would respond to me, "Yeah! There's a lot of things I don't like about this country, but you don't see me forsaking everything I hold near and dear to me and forsaking everything I believe in to go live in a former communist satellite state of the Soviet Union!" A very impassioned plea I make on your behalves out there. It's definitely thinking outside of the box.*

*There is some truth in that statement. It does weigh somewhat on my conscience, but not enough to keep me here.*

*On the one hand I am forsaking much of what I believed in as a young man.*

*I've wept many a bitter tear when specific United States teams or individuals, were vanquished by the Soviets or other Eastern block countries during the Olympics. Conversely, I have celebrated to a point just past delirium when the opposite occurred. If you would have told me when I was twelve years old (just after the Soviets stole the first Gold medal ever in basketball) that I would have chosen to live in the Ukraine some day, I would have considered you either to be a lunatic, incredibly insensitive, very stupid, or all of the above.*

## Maturity, it happens to the best of us

*But on the other hand, I'm not twelve years old anymore, and my tears then were the tears of a child who didn't know anything about what was really important in life. On the list of things to cry about, who wins a basketball (or any other game) game doesn't make it into my top one million.*

*Things change.*

*Countries change.*

*Life changes.*

*People get their hearts broken, then, they get them mended again.*

*Hopefully, people grow up, not just old.*

*I still bleed red white and blue like you do.*

## Don't let the door hit you where the good Lord split you, Tom

*I'm not completely prepared (who would be?) to pull up stakes and hand over the keys to the place to the thugs, degenerates, criminals, and corrupt politicians (These guys are the morons that will eventually be the main reason this country goes bankrupt at some point in the near future. On some level, I'm glad I won't be here when it happens, but that probably won't prevent me from saying "I told you so" either). Add to that, illegal immigrants (the other secondary cause of our financial ruination because our Southwestern border protection is like trying to stop Niagra Falls with a chain link fence. Because we do not have the financial wherewithal to feed, house, clothe and most importantly, give free medical attention to millions of people indefinitely). And the ignorant redneck slobs (people who don't feed or house or love their kids the way God said you are supposed to and would rather drink a beer and watch wrestling than play catch with their kids. Using this standard a redneck is not a geographic slur but a societal comment) who are close to becoming the cultural elite of this country.*

### It's called exodus for a good reason. They're not intended to be strolls in the park

*The exodus I was referring to earlier in the book is not only about men seeking metaphorical greener pastures with more accommodating, genteel womanly women; it will also include the average blue and white collar workers who are getting fed up more each day with how they are forced to live in this country. Higher and higher taxes, limited work opportunities (much of corporate America's workload has been outsourced to our fine Asian compadres, so if you want your old job back, all you have to do is move to Taiwan or China), cultural degradation, widespread apathy and indifference in the public schools, and on and on. This could be a five hundred page book if I elected to continue. These regular working-class Americans will be seeking out their own refuge far from the maddening crowds, the bourgeoning cookie-cutter tract suburban housing projects, and inner city war zones. Lest you think I am over dramatizing the economic, moral and social crises in America, just visit your local bookstore and pick up any current tomes on the subjects. I'm no Chicken Little trying to convince you the sky is falling, it is falling. My point of view is validated 100% by the current intellectuals, pundits, blue-blooded economists, think tank geeks, Wall Street hot shots, and Ivory Tower Ivy League prognosticators. Think of a large predator being devoured by another larger predator. That is the analogy of the economic reality of China and America. My God have you seen the footage of their factory workers, and the volume of products they churn out? It's mind blowing. From an economic standpoint it's late in the fourth quarter, the two-minute warning is approaching, and we're down by about ten touchdowns.*

### Revolution has such a harsh connotation, doesn't it?

*Some of the greatest minds in this country, have even gone so far as to suggest revolution is the only practical resolution to our problems. They make a strong case that when a country reaches the direst of straits (America?), mild reform measures are hopelessly futile, and overtly ludicrous. Really, what is the point of society in general being mildly less pathetic, degenerate, and self-destructive? The missing ingredient in the equation is cognizance.*

### Critical mass as an agent of social change

*Denial is a horrible thing. Unbelievably (at least this is what my favorite statistician tells me), only two percent of the general population believe we are in need of wholesale societal changes.*

*Well . . . all I can say to the other 98% of the people, is that somebody needs to pinch your asses so you can finally realize this is no dream. This country is going down the toilet with one mighty flush, and whether you believe it or not, is hardly the point. Yes, everybody is certainly entitled to their own opinions, just not their own facts. I am speaking in factual, not emotional terms. For example, America is bankrupt, this is an example of a fact, not an opinion.*

*It's not just China and India either. The new BRIC nations will soon dominate the world's economic landscape. At least fifty percent of the companies whose products you use in America today are now subsidiaries of these countries.*

*I don't know whether to laugh or cry.*

## Galileo now demonstrates the incredible obvious instead of the merely obvious

*It reminds me of the story about Galileo. It was reported that when he dropped objects of various weights from the top of the Leaning Tower of Pisa and they hit the ground at the same time, the people scoffed at him. Even after seeing the objects hit the ground at the same time with their own eyes. They assumed it to be a clever trick an optical illusion, much like his devil's scepter (telescope for you civilians out there) that he was using to divine some of the previously unknown secrets of the solar system. What, you mean the moon isn't a crystal sphere, and the sun doesn't revolve around the Earth?*

## Be careful who you select as your patron, you may end up looking like an idiot some day

*Aristotle had already convinced the Catholic Church almost two thousand years earlier about the nature of falling bodies (heavier objects are attracted to the earth at a greater rate) and the Earth-centered solar system. Who was this clever mathematician to defy Aristotle?*

*What do you expect the masses to believe when presented with conflicting information: ritualized church-sponsored dogma, or the truth?*

*Denial, I tell you.*

*No, I don't have to hand over the keys to the place, neither do you. They already have the keys.*

*I don't leave without fear or trepidation. These are natural human emotions. I just want something better than what I have. I had to eat the same pile of shit off of a plate* for most of my life in America. I would rather not comment on who was serving it to me. Gentleman to the end, I say. I almost got to the point I liked the taste of it. But not quite!

## The least you could do is sauté my crow before I have to eat it

Will I end up back in America after a few weeks or months like a whipped pup with my tail between my legs? Maybe.

Could I be wrong about the Ukraine? Of course. But don't bet anymore than you can afford to lose on that being true.

Of course I could do the safe thing and stay here, never find out if I would have made it or not. I could be an old man lying on my deathbed someday saying to myself, "I should've gone . . . I should've at least tried."

In all honesty, my bets have been hedged slightly by my fellow Ukrainian Knight, Lance, whom I have sent ahead of me.

Lance is no coward for leaving America. He is not turning from the fracas or giving up the fight. If anything, he is the bravest man I know.

## Lance wears a lot of hats

He is not only my best friend, but he is my role model and guru as I've mentioned before. The job doesn't pay much, unless of course you count my friendship. Like I said, it doesn't pay much.

On top of that paltry pay, I know that Lance has given much more of himself as my friend the last couple of years, than he has ever received from me. There is your definition of a friend in case you were looking for one.

I didn't actually send Lance anywhere. He is after all a very big boy, quite capable of making his own decisions, with or without my influence and self-serving propaganda.

Lance did what most of you would consider an unthinkable, irrational, and downright self-destructive. At first glance you might even think it to be the action of a mad man. But my fellow Ukrainian Knight and best friend likes to quote an old song, "Freedom's just another word for nothing left to lose."

When you have nothing left to lose and everything to gain, why not take a chance?

### Everybody makes a last stand somewhere, at some point in their lives

If he loses the gamble he ends up back in America, no worse off than he was when he left or he gives another country the chance to bring in the dark horse, I would consider it "all victory," to quote an old crony of mine. It looks like a win/win proposition from where I'm sitting.

Before Lance left this country, he had an estate sale. He sold off everything he owned, except for a few prized possessions he left in my care. Yes, it has a "burning-the-bridge" air about it, maybe even slightly reckless (I was thinking to myself that he might want some of that stuff back at some point in the future), but it also has an aura of symmetry to it, also. Not to belabor the point too much but life is like a circle. In order to complete the circle, some things will have *to be discarded along the way. Some of them are things; sadly, some of them are people.*

*The preconceived ideations and the precognitive notions that most of us have are mighty obstacles. Since we've already danced to that tune, let us not do it again.*

*What Lance has done, and I am about to do, are not the circles of everyone's life. It's just the one that for better, or worse, we have chosen.*

## You know what the generals always say about the first reports from battle

*The first reports from the Ukraine are very, very encouraging. Lance's descriptive words include illusions to paradise and Heaven. Is he exaggerating? Probably not.*

*Lance may be using paradise and Heaven as relative terms. Life in the Ukraine, may be paradise and Heaven, compared to living in America. Americans certainly don't want these things to be true.*

*We've made up our minds, don't confuse us with reality. Because there is a patriotic soul that dwells within all of us, we choose to believe that we will never have life as good anywhere in the world as we have it right here.*

## If they know so much, why are they always crazy?

*Psychologists will tell you that to just perceive an idea or to maintain a perceived belief or notion (albeit a false one) about anything, will put you one step closer to achieving this vision. If you perceive that America is the land of milk and honey, you're half way there. The idea is a first cousin to the commonly help expression that your perception of reality is the only reality that should matter to you. Never mind that your belief is not based on something that is actually real. That's just a detail.*

*Good luck!*

### With the right seasonings, it really isn't that bad

*I call my friend often. I get the distinct feeling that Lance would never live in America again. He may have toiled in the valley most of his life, he may have lived in obscurity, he may have supped at the same plate I have, he may have had an unrewarding, meaningless, joyless and sometimes mundane existence while he was here, but he's been to the mountain now. I doubt he ever wants to come back to the valley. To the land of ash heaps Fitzgerald wrote so beautifully about. Maybe his experiences could be filed under the slogan, "Once they've been to the big city, you can't keep them down on the farm." Or more succinctly, to the postulation that there really are greener pastures out there if you can just find the right fence to look over.*

*Lance is an English teacher.*

*His job is not any more difficult than having conversations (hence the title, conversational English) with very beautiful and fascinating women. Although there are* **some** *men in his classes; this happens to be a particularly revolting development that he is in no way encouraging.*

*He tells me his job is so easy he would gladly pay them for the opportunity to teach his classes if they asked him to. Ever hear an American teacher offer to pay the school for the honor of teaching American kids?*

*I know it sounds maudlin, but I realize Lance is in a better place now. The Ukraine is a country almost perfectly suited to his philosophy, temperament, and lifestyle.*

## A prophet hath no honor in his own country

*It s the perfect example of a man with an exquisite talent (enchanting beautiful women with his rapier wit) finding the right avenue (Ukraine) to let his talent blossom to it's fullest measure.*

*I feel like I am learning at an exponential rate now. Not only do I have my own experiences in the Ukraine to draw from, I am corresponding with some Ukrainians, as well as visiting with Lance about his experiences. And I will soon be at least a part time citizen of the Ukraine.*

*I suppose there is a finite amount of things to be gleaned from the familiar.*

*I've lived in the finite world long enough. I've feasted on the crumbs that have fallen from the table of this existentialist dream/nightmare world in America long enough.*

## Essentially, I'm just trading out the size of my pond

*I have lived in the same town (notwithstanding a few years on a military installation, multiple colleges, and escapades abroad) for practically my entire life. My influences and educational opportunities were essentially static. While I have ventured forth from my pond occasionally, it has most certainly not been enough times to alter my vision or my sensibilities in any significant way.*

*So it is finally time that this chapter of my life and this book draw to an end. I am already looking forward (with great zest and zeal) to writing my next installment.*

*But I shall rest for a season.*

*Who knows T.S. Elliot may prove to be the prophet of the hour after all. That after venturing forth into the great unknown (seeking out that thing which I didn't have), I will arrive where I started and know myself and my country or countries for the first time.*

# Epilogue

*The saddest part of my life in America was not that I had a meaningless joyless existence like Lance had. I talk to so many people now that tell me they don't know of a single happy person in America. It didn't use to be this way. Our parent's generation was happier. We are definitely doing something wrong. That was definitely not the saddest part. The saddest part of it all was that I didn't even know it. I also had so many possessions I eventually discovered I either had a possession fetish, or a possession sickness.*

*Like the man who grows up in the house that has water in his basement that slowly but surely fills up his entire house until one day he drowns. He just assumed everything was fine because he had never known anything else. Do what you can with what you have in the time you have with where you are. Are you doing that now? You may only get one shot at life. Make sure it's your best shot. People who get to the end of their lives always regret what they didn't do, never what they did do; well, assuming they weren't an axe murderer or a Democrat, of course.*

*How much time do you spend contemplating your mortality?*

*I know that sometimes life seems too long. Like when you are waiting to go on a trip like I did to the Ukraine. Sometimes life seems too short, like every minute I spent in the Ukraine.*

*You may be the most content soul in the world. You may have a loving family, a great job, great friends, and a cottage on the beach. Good for you. The American dream worked out for you. Nice!*

*Just remember what I said about the possibilities.*

*I don't want to insult anyone's intelligence out there, but the trip I am embarking on is my personal journey of discovering the world. Surely, you don't think I believe my journey is the only one worthy to undertake. Your journey might be something just as grand, but you might take a decidedly different route.*

*There are several trails you can take to get to a mountain top.*

*The great crooner George Strait had a nice line in one of his songs. To paraphrase George, "God intended for us to venture forth from the sands of our own shore and once we get to another land and scale that mountain, the first ones to sing, will be the last ones who said they wanted to go." I don't know about you, but I don't argue with George Strait. If he said it or sung about it, I believe it.*

*I don't know what your motivations are, or where your passions lie. Maybe you want to live thirty years in the African bush like Jane Goodall or maybe you want to sail around the world or climb Mt. Everest. All of these ideas are certainly worthy goals. My only advice to you is that you better not wait too long. Or you will wake up one day and decide you are that old person who no longer wants to do what you always wanted to do. The only thing you have to look forward to in your golden years, is sitting in your recliner drooling on yourself and eventually crapping in your pants, all the time dreaming of old used-to-be's and what might-have-been's. You will have to go stand in line with the rest of the old people, and just wait. Wait for the end. In the years since I've been divorced (living in the real world now) I have learned just how flawed people are, and how bad human nature can be. I've seen grave injustices done against my fellow man in the name of unholy crusades.*

*I've been witness to and participated in what most of you would label as outrageous and outlandish behavior. Not criminal, just not anything to brag about.*

*I've seen the lowest forms of humanity and how sometimes they are forced to eek out a miserable existence doing things none of you would even consider doing.*

*I've seen the elite and privileged class of different societies (rich Americans and Europeans who were uncultured, unsophisticated, uncouth and completely classless) and observed how their behavior can be just as reprehensible and despicable as a common criminal's behavior is.*

*But, I've also seen uncommon grace and kindness and tenderness of affection from people living in the most undesirable conditions.*

*I've seen generosity, benevolence and compassion from those people in society who would be considered the downtrodden and least of us.*

*I see the world with my eyes completely open now. While it's true, I can't explain everything that happens in my environment, and I'm no closer to understanding women then I've ever been in my life, at least I'm headed in the right direction. I'm going forward now. While my vision is still hampered by my somewhat inefficient filtering system I see well enough to know that you can still have a wonderful life if you are willing to try a little harder, and the world is mostly a beautiful place to live. We may as well finish with something Fitzgerald said about one of his fictional characters, Dick Diver. In the book Tender is the Night, fate and the character's own human weaknesses conspired against him, to bring about his downfall. Fitzgerald wryly noted that, "He had to live the rest of his life with the knowledge that at one time in his life he could have been something."*

Well, so can you.

# *Epilogue II*

*In the interim period after I finished my book and sent it to the editor for a final appraisal, I went back to the Ukraine to look for a place to relocate permanently. I am now retired and intent on doing just what I said I would do. Live out at least part of my days in the Ukraine. Since I am a retired teacher, it's logical that I continue to ply my trade (in a roundabout way) as a conversational English teacher.*

*I do have another reason to go back to the Ukraine. That reason's name is Marina. It might be fair to subtitle the chapter on our Malta adventure as "A Story with no Heroes".*

*Well, except for Dima. He was the very definition of the innocent bystander. Certainly, he was a central figure in the tale, but he was carried along by the action of the plot, he never precipitated the action. Like a sailboat anchored in Mellaha bay, Dima was moved about by the forces that surrounded him.*

*I tried to relate the incidents on the trip as honestly as I could, but we all know that each of us perceives events in our lives, through our own fuzzy filters.*

*Once again I flew off into the great unknown that is the Ukraine. To an uncertain fate, and an uncertain future.*

*I landed in Kiev, hooked up with a fiery interpreter friend, Sobina (who I adore because she insists on drinking vodka shots at the oddest times of the day, like for instance when the sun comes up, the sun goes down, and the in between time as well,) at the airport and took a cab ride into Kiev Square. We had a fantastic buffet, and walked around the main square until it was time to catch our train. We had to take an overnight train ride (the first time I had ever been on a train) from Kiev to Dnepropetrovsk.*

*We arrived around 7:00am the next morning and caught a trombline to Lance's flat.*

*I spent the next several days brooding and skulking about the main square searching my heart for just the right words to say to Marina, and of course the courage to confront Marina.*

*I debated whether I should see her at all hundreds of times in my own mind. It was easy to make a strong case to support any conclusion I reached. Marina had her chances to show me how she felt, and she squandered those chances in Malta. On the other hand, in Malta, I was obviously overloaded by the unfamiliar surroundings and the language barriers of the main players, including the local Italian populace. Besides, my ineptitude at getting things done at least made me partially culpable in some of our troubles.*

*My courage rose and fell like wallflowers at a high school dance.*

*As I stood on the balcony of the eight story flat I shared with Lance, gazing across the mighty breadth of the Dnepr River, the July wind was whipping through my hair. I could see the lights of one of the four main bridges that crossed the Dnepr reflecting off of the water like giant fireworks sparklers. I could make out the fireworks display half way across the river until the light finally dimmed into a dark oblivion. I was taking measured sips (a no no in the Ukraine) of my fine Ukrainian vodka pondering my immediate future, and if I should even see Marina at all. There was little to gain, much to lose from an encounter with Marina.*

*I delayed the inevitable for as long as possible the next day. I finally drug myself into the Hotel Central, the same hotel where I first sought out a new direction for my life. What I have already said about our first social at the restaurant on the Dnepr River was true. But, equally as profound of an impact on my psyche was the morning after my first night in the Hotel Central when I looked out of my window onto Bolshoi Lenin below me. All I could say to myself was that I should have gotten here sooner. I've missed out on too much living. My days are not nearly over, but I've wallowed in the Spring, Summer is a fading memory, and now Fall has arrived.*

*To refresh our collective memories, Marina works in an office on the fourth floor of the hotel doing translations for foreign men involved in either business transactions, or formal introductions for non-english speaking local Ukrainian girls.*

*I wandered up to the outer office and just sat there for a few moments, rehearsing my speech in my head. What would her reaction to seeing me again be? Warm, neutral, cold, scornful, perfunctory, or possibly violent? I had already suffered two major injuries at the hands of Marina, one to my leg and the other to my buttocks muscle (which had never healed properly, because I still have a slight limp) in separate lovemaking accidents with her. I could only imagine what kind of damage she would do to me if she were actually intending to hurt me.*

*But, it was much ado about nothing. Marina greeted me in a pleasant manner and even seemed happy to see me again. My heart was doing summersaults inside of my chest. Damn heart, stop that!*

*After a few minutes of talking, Marina silently retreated to her office and then miraculously (as if conjuring him up out of thin air) reappeared with the magnificent Dima at her side. I was close to an emotional breakdown now. Boy, had he grown in one year, but still ever bit as handsome and charming as I remembered.*

*So, it was a glad reunion day.*

*Marina wanted to go out for dinner that night. That was an encouraging development. Although I wasn't quite sure how I felt about revisiting a road I had journeyed down before only to find sadness at the end.*

*I picked Marina up that night after work in front of the Hotel Central. We got into a taxi and she gave instructions to the driver in Russian.*

*It was a long ride. I instantly recognized the restaurant. It was the very same restaurant where I had proposed to Marina and gave her the ring the previous summer. So, little Marina does have some sentimentality left in her bones for old Tom. She wished to revisit the night of all nights and possibly re-inact "Fireworks on the Dnepr." Maybe, she is going to explain her actions in Malta. Maybe profess her undying love for me, and tell me she has been miserable without me. Or at the very least tell me why I fell out of favor with her.*

*It was another wonderful dinner. We devoured course after course. By the time we had drank our way to the bottom of a really dry red wine, Marina had morphed into the old Marina. The one that had captured my heart on my first go around here. I truly love Marina's company. The truth is that when we are together alone she is in girlfriend mode very deeply. With Dima around, like in Malta, I am more like furniture in the restaurant, essential to the meal of course, but certainly not an overriding concern. It took one more time of being with Marina to figure this out. I was very disappointed in myself. That I didn't understand something that was so simple, so elementary, that was right in front of me all along. I have after all been a father for almost twenty years. The maternal instinct isn't an overly complicated concept to understand. It's not like explaining Astrophysics to a supermodel. The bottom line is that I had incredible expectations about the trip to Malta. I had built the trip up to be nothing much more than an extended romantic interlude that I had mentioned earlier in the book.*

*It was unfair and kind of childish to expect more than Marina gave to me in Malta. Dima was wonderful, but he was a handful, Marina was constantly dressing him for different adventures and excursions, and cleaning and grooming him, all at the same time having to maintain a passionate relationship with me. I should have realized this at the time. I shouldn't have held Maria to the Dnepropetrovsk standard of conduct that she is still so clearly willing and able to maintain.*

*I was surprised at how mature Marina and I discussed Malta. Marina was shocked that I felt the way I said I did. She claimed to have been experiencing female problems on the night in question. At least that's what she claimed. She was even more shocked that I left without saying goodbye to her. I said at the time I should have taken the high ground. I was just too hurt at the time. It now seems possible that the hurt I was feeling (at Marina's slights) was a product of my ample imagination, and not correlated very well to Marina's actions, or the actual events that had taken place in Malta. Sometimes people can spend too much time analyzing their lives, and every single thing that happens to them, and not enough time just living their lives.*

*At the end of the evening, Marina invited me to go with her and Dima to Crimea the very next weekend. Which is the Black Sea region of the Ukraine. Almost every Ukrainian vacations in the Black Sea, every summer. It has close to a Mediterranean climate. Majestic mountains, lush vegetation, and is sparsely populated. Crimea has the feel of an Italian seaside village. Slow pace, peaceful, hardly any work going on, and friendlier people than most of the Ukraine. Most Ukrainian cities are full of bustle in the same way most big cities are. People aren't trying to be rude, they just have things to do and sometimes you are in their way.*

*I met Marina and Dima on the steps of the train station. It took several hours to secure tickets (an elaborate process in the Ukraine) and finally climb on board the train.*

*It was another overnight train. While Marina lay down to sleep, Dima and I slipped out of our compartments, ostensibly to find a bathroom. I held him up to the open window of the train. As the train thundered down the tracks we were treated to a brilliantly white moon reflecting off of the Dnepr river on a cloudless Ukrainian night. The last time I had seen a child smile that big was my own children at Christmas. The whole scene was right out of a movie. Every few miles we would cross a spectacular rickety bridge that I had imagined carried troops (many to their doom I suppose) and armaments back in World War Two (The Great Patriotic War for my Russian friends out there) to fend off Hitler's advances. Most of Hitler's atrocities against the Russian people were committed in Ukrainian cities, like Kiev, and Sevastopal.*

*It was an interminable train ride.*

*We pulled into Alushta around 6:45am the next morning. After disembarking from the train, the three of us were mobbed by local taxi drivers trying to persuade us (or actually Marina), to take their cab and not somebody else's.*

*My status as an American citizen (my American style of clothes and dark hair gives me away) ensured that we would have attention (because of course they assume all Americans have mucho Grivnas) wherever we chanced to make an appearance. Call it the Bill Gates.*

*Marina finally settled on an older man, who after loading our luggage into the trunk proceeded to take us to visit many hotels in Alushta, until Marina found just the right one with the right accommodations, view, and price. Marina was in no hurry. It took hours to find just the right place to stay. A ten-unit hotel with a view of the mountains in one direction and the Black Sea in the other. There was also a courtyard covered in cherry trees and grapes, and a beautiful Sharpei who paroled the grounds like a benevolent house detective. He would come in and out of the rooms at will checking up on his tenants as he saw fit. I believe Ukrainians savor the process of selecting hotels and meals and excursions as much as the actual things themselves.*

*We unloaded our luggage, changed into beachwear and flip-flops and headed off for an impromptu dinner and stroll on the beach. One of the most remarkable things about the Ukraine in my mind, is that just when you thought you've seen everything, or tasted everything, you get surprised. We had a great meal, which consisted of some items I had never seen or heard of before, despite my vast experience dining in the Ukraine. Forget about processed food. With fruit trees in abundance, vineyards surrounding the entire valley, and the Black Sea at arms reach, everything is fresh.*

*I have a theory, not backed up by anything but personal observation (other than the one fact almost thirty countries in the world community have chosen not to import food from America due to the supposed hormone levels, and diversity of additives and preservatives which permeates our food) that the food in America is killing us. Cancer used to be a fairly rare occurrence in the younger population. Not anymore. Why? Maybe it's our contaminated food?*

*Or maybe it's because I'm getting older and it just seems like everyone is dying from cancer.*

*After dinner we walked down by the Black Sea. It was getting dusky. The boardwalk surrounding the water was marble. Incredible. The side of the boardwalk was perfectly manicured with all kinds of trees and shrubs. Crimea was shaping up to be a very big deal.*

*The three of us forced a retreat back to our hotel as the sun slowly made it's perilous descent out of sight.*

*What I am about to tell you is just an informational point. A little tidbit that might throw even more illumination on the cultural differences between Americans and Ukrainians. Marina was already thinking about what to do for breakfast the next morning. There were excursions planned and we were not about to wander around the city wiling away the hours looking for breakfast. Marina performed an obviously incalculable operation in her head and told me to do the following. Actually she showed me what to do, to eliminate any chance of miscommunication. She told me to hold Dima's hand and she began to walk at a very slow pace in front of us. She stopped after about ten or fifteen feet and told me to walk at the same speed straight ahead. She then said that I would be able to turn either to the left or the right. She said turn to the left keeping up the same pace for two streets. Then turn right and continue. She would catch up to us after she had purchased breakfast items at the grocery store. Amazing. My first thought was why not just sit on a bench and wait for her outside of the grocery store? Answer. It's a waste of time when we could be doing something productive, that's why.*

*I did just what she asked me to, and she indeed caught up to Dima and me, just a few blocks from our hotel.*

*For you quick studies out there, don't get ahead of me. You already know what is in my immediate future.*

*A rude awakening. Which is what I always call having to get out of bed.*

*But to quote a very old cliché it was like dejavu all over again when Marina opened my hotel room the next morning and uttered the now famous words "Five minutes, Tom, we eat in five minutes." What? No pre-breakfast swim in the Black Sea? Which by the way is a hell of a lot colder in June, than the Mediterranean is in mid July. I felt like I had been spared the executioner's blade by avoiding the pre-breakfast swim. It seemed to me that Marina was getting mellow in her old age. Lucky for me.*

*So, that morning we had a lovely breakfast on our hotel veranda as the sum rose slowly over the not so distant mountains.*

*That days activities would turn out to be the best excursion of our trip to Crimea. We met a van that was already filled with a bunch of Ukrainians. We were headed up to the mountains for a horseback ride. It was not to be your typical perfunctory tourist horseback ride you would receive at a resort in the American west. Like at a dude ranch. I've been on those before. They provided riding clothes and matched our horses and gear to each of us individually. We rode the horses for hours on end on steep mountain trails. We frequently rested the horses and watered and fed them. This was an all day affair. At a mid-way point we dismounted and were fed a campfire type meal and went on a hike up into the steeper part of the mountains. Solid Conglomerate formations jutted out from everywhere. Never before had I seen conglomerates the size of houses. Usually they are the size of baseballs. It was quite spectacular. The clouds, which were high overhead when we began our ride, were now on top of us. We were literally walking and riding horses in the clouds. It was cool at this altitude, but not cold. I was almost praying for death to take me, because I knew my life could only go downhill after this point in time. Oh, if we could only grasp the rapture and joy of these moments in our lives, and keep them with us always. What a life it would be. Moonlight Graham once said "hardly anyone can recognize the significant events in their lives as they are happening, they just brush by us like the wind."*

*Eventually, the ride did end and we returned back to base camp. We then had the Ukrainian version of a campfire sing along with plenty of spirits and good food. What a day.*

*The next day was not so exciting for either Marina or myself, but boy did Dima love it. We spent the entire day at a water park. It was organized exactly like an American water park. With floaties, food vendors, and lots of people who had no business wearing either speedos or thongs. Egads!*

*The next couple of days were spent on excursions of the surrounding countryside. One day it would be the vineyards. Wow, you have not had wine until you have had Crimean wine. You would relegate all French wine as mouthwash, after drinking this liquid golden concotion.*

*The next day it would be a tour of Sevastopal. The Ukrainian equivalent of our Pearl Harbor, with Germany playing the role of Japan. Sevastopal has incredible war memorials and monuments. And they should. Sevastopalan's have a rich and famous history.*

*They apparently fought against the Nazis as courageously (almost singlehandedly holding off the might* of the Wermarcht) as any city could have that was under constant bombardment.

We spent one entire day on the beach. Just getting wet, and frolicking in the sand. It's mostly rocky though, very little sand. Just like Malta.

Marina was in mother mode once again. The obvious difference between this vacation and Malta, was my level of expectations were more reasonable.

On our last day we took an excursion to Yalta. Yes, the same Yalta where the big three (Churchill, Stalin, and Roosevelt) met during World War Two. So, I have now been to Yalta and Malta. There really isn't anything funny or intriguing about that historical fact, other than it has a nice ring to it, I suppose.

We must have walked a hundred miles on this trip. Through vineyards, hiking up mountain passes, on the beach, in the parks, and on the boardwalk.

It was blissful, and I was content.

However, (as I am sure you have duly noted), Marina and I were not engaging in any romantic interludes. The conversations we had were pleasant and often animated, and she frequently gave me history lessons on the long-suffering nature of her people, and of her country (she was right) as opposed to the spoiled Americans who have remained relatively unscathed throughout modern history. Obviously, we have no ancient history. A fact she frequently reminded me about.

But, we were like two old high school lovers resigned to just being friends. Our romantic fate was sealed the previous summer, by events that were not in our overt control or even within our complete capacity to understand either.

I wasn't bitter because I wasn't able to re-ignite our romance. On the contrary, I was happy to see her, and

*Dima of course. I felt like I was already making good on my promise to Dima.*

*I spent what was left of my last night in Crimea tossing and turning. I had big ideas coming here. They weren't realized of course, but I was truly grateful for a chance to redeem myself, even if in some small way.*

*I couldn't help myself. Just like in Malta when I went down to the hotel bar to chat with the old guy (of course this time around, I had no romantic tale to regale anyone with, and there was no bar with an old guy, just the cleaning lady) and then make my way to the Sea.*

*It was the same level of blackness as the Mediterranean Sea. It still produced the same feelings of euphoria and dread as the Mediterranean Sea did for me last summer. The Black Sea sleeps just as peacefully in the Earth's arms as the Mediterranean Sea does.*

*I didn't feel so bad this time.*

*I still couldn't rewrite the tale and switch out the happy ending where the boy and girl ride off into the sunset, but at least I wasn't grasping at hope and yesterday anymore. I also like the fairy tale where the princess has to kiss a lot of frogs before she finds her prince. Well, I'll have you know I have had to kiss way more than my share of ungodly gorgeous young Ukrainian supermodels these last couple of years to find my one princess, and it is a task that I am proud to say I am still carrying out with the stiffest of upper lips, and most serious of intentions. So . . . I will carry on with this grueling task*

*A wise man once told me this about relationships. I have no idea if it is original to him, or if he borrowed it from someone else.*

*Before you can begin again you have to have a good ending.*

*Marina and I had a lovely ending.*

*Now, I can go forward.*

*Now, I can live again, without the shadows of my mind, or even the cloudy darkness that hovers always just outside of human comprehension to taunt my dreamless nights. It feels so good just to have dreams again. And yes, my dreams center around mostly Ukrainian girls and vodka and me trying to impress them somehow.*

*It was to be my last day in Dnepropetrovsk before I headed back to America. As luck would have it I happened to be riding the trombine on the very day they dropped the young cottonwood saplings into their new homes on Karl Marx Boulevard.*

*In a remarkable twist of fate, or kismet, or divine intervention I ran into Dorian Gray. Not THE Dorian Gray, but the Dnepropetrovsk version. As wise, dapper, and well-heeled as any gentlemen you will ever meet in your life. In the absence of my old friend Lance, who unexpectedly returned to America due to homesickness, he is my new companion, and dare I say it, life long.*

*He serves as my confidant and esteemed mentor.*

*On the night I met him he was walking down Karl Marxa boulevard with very attractive girls on both arms. Always a good sign I say.*

*Which happened to be standard practice for Dorian as I subsequently learned. He has taken me under his wing, and his divine tutelage, and I have decided what life I have left, will be spent with him now.*

*When I left America I left a lot of friends behind. But I had the good fortune to bring one with me. He is now gone, but, what was that old expression, "when one door closes, another one opens. To take great liberties and paraphrase my favorite writer "to lose one friend is considered bad fortune, to lose them all, merely carelessness."*

*I will cling to this one and try my best not to lose him along the way.*

*As I was saying about the saplings.*

*They were impossibly slender and frail looking.*

*I thought to myself they'll never survive the first long siege of a real Russian winter. Their roots won't be deep enough, nor their bark thick enough to survive the killing frosts to come. I also told my riding companion, Dorian, that one day in the distant future, maybe in thirty years when I have entered my own winter of days, that I will once again revisit this very spot, and hopefully these tender willowy saplings will have grown majestic, noble, tall, and sturdy. They will have rooted themselves very deeply in the dark Ukrainian soil, and have barks so thick that only a chain saw or axe could do them any real harm. A famous line from an old American country song tells us, "Old oaks and old folks stand tall, just pretend."*

*To wit, "Learn to live well, play well, love well, eat and drink your fill, walk sober off before a sprightlier age comes tittering on and shows you from the stage. Alexander Pope.*

*There is no pretending in real life, only in songs, movies, and other such fantasy, is fate such a wonderful friend. I will wait for summer to give the cottonwoods in all of their glory and bluster time to put on one full coat of colors one last time.*

*I will hobble aboard the trombline, (hopefully with Dorian, or my impossibly gorgeous wife, or both) and take one last ride up Karl Marx Boulevard past these grand old trees. Who knows, maybe I'll even say a quite goodbye to the trees underneath my breath. The saplings of my early old age will now be defiant sentinels of my last golden years.*

*I hope that when this day arrives, and it surely will, that I can muster all of the grace and magnanimity of my soul and spirit (holding no malevolence in my heart for their grand age and days to come) and be happy that the trees of my elder youth did in fact survive all of those cruel Russian winters.*

*And as I step off that trombline for the last time and turn my back on Karl Marx Boulevard, (but never to Dorian) to complete what is left of my journey here in the Ukraine and on Earth I hope that I am thankful that my life did happen, and that I lived and loved well, that I was a good father, husband, and friend; and that I won't be too sad that it's now over.*

*The first ending of this book, in Malta, was decidedly sad and unfulfilling. Although I realize it was certainly the more natural ending, or stopping point, and had a certain poignancy to it; I hate sad endings with all of my soul. This last ending is much more suitable and fulfilling, and it has that rarest of all qualities in a good book, it's very true.*

*I have now regrettably told the tale in all of it's glory, with most of the gory tales left to your imaginations, and I really really hope you have good imaginations. A final thought, I wish all of my fellow Ukrainian Knights out there, past, present, and future, good luck and Godspeed.*